UNDENIABLE SOLIDARITY

How Dogs and Humans Domesticated One Another

David Hagner, Ph.D.

authorHOUSE®

AuthorHouse™
1663 Liberty Drive
Bloomington, IN 47403
www.authorhouse.com
Phone: 1 (800) 839-8640

Published by AuthorHouse 08/27/2018

ISBN: 978-1-5462-5638-0 (sc)
ISBN: 978-1-5462-5637-3 (hc)
ISBN: 978-1-5462-5636-6 (e)

Library of Congress Control Number: 2018909909

Print information available on the last page.

This book is printed on acid-free paper.

For
Spook: 1963 – 1972
Maggie: 1976 – 1984
Addie: 1997 – 2014
and
Poco the Wonder-Dog: 2015 -

CONTENTS

PREFACE

Dogs are more than pets. They are our companions and our partners, and our partnership with them has helped make us who we are. This book tells the extraordinary story of how that came about.

Few of us nowadays worry about animal predators (except other humans). But stories and legends passed down for countless generations tell of a time when they were a real threat. When the story of "Little Red Riding Hood" was first told to children living in the Black Forest region of Germany, wolves really were big and bad. You couldn't go visit your grandmother without worrying about them.

But a good solution to the problem was brought to us, ironically, by several of the wolves themselves. They suggested that we let them live with us and give them scraps of our delicious cooked food, and in return, they would make sure we stayed safe. The rest, as they say, is history.

And it's a very long history; so long, in fact, that our two species have undergone biological changes over the millennia as we adapted to one another. The secure feeling we get when man's best friend is near us is by now hard-wired into our biology. And the wolves who came to live with us have become a special sub-species of wolf called dogs.

It is no wonder, then, that therapy and service dogs are used so often today to help calm and heal people in distress. They are masters at that. But only a few decades ago, most people refused to believe that such a thing was possible. They dismissed the idea as too good to be true.

In my work as a rehabilitation counselor, and later a university professor, I witnessed the powerful effects of therapy and service dogs, and I too could scarcely believe it. After all, a lot of the time a therapy dog pretty much just lies there and naps. Nice work if you can get it!

When I retired from full-time work and had free time, I set about investigating what makes therapy dogs effective. The more I learned, the more fascinating the story became. And the explanation turned out to be more amazing than I could ever have predicted. Curl up with your dog and read all about it.

1

Therapy Tails

There are no human communities without dogs. The first Europeans to explore New Zealand could not find any dogs there, and so they assumed at first that the native Maori people were an exception. But as they came to understand and communicate with the Maori people, they learned that the Maori originally brought dogs with them on their long outrigger canoes when they first populated New Zealand's two islands. But at one point, a particularly difficult famine had forced their starving ancestors to use their dogs for food or perish themselves. Dogs accompanied the European explorers, and today dogs are as plentiful in New Zealand as everywhere else.

We have taken dogs with us wherever we went. The day after the Mayflower landed in Plymouth, Massachusetts in November, 1620, a couple of passengers ventured out from the ship, led by captain Myles Standish and accompanied by one of the two dogs on board. Later that day, some other passengers also went ashore, and saw some men with a dog, whom they assumed were the other party from their ship. But as they got closer they realized these people were Native Americans, who took off into the forest, whistling their dog after them. Dogs had accompanied humans across the Bering Strait to North America more than 15,000 years previously and were an important part of every Native American community.

It is no surprise, then, that the bond between dogs and humans is extraordinarily close. The vast majority of people respond positively to the presence of a dog. This response seems to be amplified for people who are experiencing difficulties, such as those who are socially isolated or are coping with pain or with a disability, and is sometimes so striking as to be scarcely believable. While I have enjoyed having a dog as part of my family since I was a young child, I began to be seriously interested in the dog/human relationship through my work as a rehabilitation counselor with therapy and service dogs and their impact on people with disabilities.

Investigation of the therapeutic role of dogs has its roots in the work of Dr. Boris Levinson in the late 1950s with children with emotional difficulties. Dr. Levinson sometimes let his dog Jingles accompany him to his New York City therapy practice because Jingles preferred this to spending the day alone. Jingles would simply lie on the floor and nap. But Dr. Levinson soon noticed that many of the children he was treating made more progress in therapy on the days when when Jingles was in the room. To test this further, he began routinely introducing Jingles to his patients, and unless the child was afraid of dogs, including Jingles in the sessions.

Usually Jingles was just there as an observer, but sometimes a child got down on the floor and cuddled up to him, or preferred rolling around and playing with him to sitting still, and Jingles was happy to oblige. Some children also talked to Jingles. Dr. Levinson noticed that they would sometimes say deeply personal things to Jingles that they found it too difficult to say to a human.

Dr. Levinson took notes on the positive effect Jingles had on his patients, and he presented a paper about it at a professional psychology conference. He suggested that dogs might have value as "co-therapists" in the treatment of children with emotional difficulties. But instead of responding with interest and fascination, the scientific community at the time rejected his findings as preposterous and refused to take him seriously, responding instead with wisecracks like "How much does the dog charge?"

That might have been the end of the matter. There might be no therapy dogs today. But coincidently, Dr. Levinson presented his findings about 20 years after the death of Sigmund Freud, just as Freud's letters were being collected, translated and published by his son Ernst. As people interested in Freud began reading his letters, they were amazed to discover how important Freud believed his dog was to the development of the psychoanalytic method.

There was no mention of dogs in any of Freud's formal papers or books, but he wrote about his observations in some of his private letters. Freud sometimes brought his dog – a chow-chow named Jofi – into psychoanalysis sessions, because the dog liked accompanying him, like Jingles with Boris Levinson. Freud slowly began to sense that Jofi could help him understand a patient's state of mind. If a patient was stressed or anxious, Jofi would lie a little further away than usual. If the person was depressed, Jofi would lie right next to the psychoanalyst's couch.

Freud then began to notice that the Jofi's presence seemed beneficial to his patients. It helped them feel more calm and relaxed, and this gave them the strength to work harder through difficult points in their analysis, such as when bringing into consciousness a repressed conflict or a painful memory.

1. Sigmund Freud and Jofi, 1937

In the 1950s and 1960s Freud had a powerful influence on the therapeutic professions, so his newly published letters were widely read and discussed. As a result, the scientific community gradually became open to the possibility that Boris Levinson might be onto something and dogs might have therapeutic value. This eventually prompted research studies that affirmed the therapeutic effect of a dog. In one of the happy coincidences of history, Freud's minor writings helped legitimize the work of Boris Levinson and Jingles, and therapy and service dogs have now become an important complement to many types of human services.

The scientific literature has now overwhelmingly validated positive therapeutic effects of dogs in a variety of contexts. The reporting of positive results by independent research teams using different research protocols has confirmed that the use of therapy and service dogs is an evidence-based practice, and it is now used extensively. A look at some of the most important studies shows several examples of these positive effects and provides a solid foundation for what follows. (But if reading about research bores you, feel free to skip the next section.)

Therapy Dog Effectiveness

A therapy dog is a dog who is brought into a treatment setting and used as part of a service plan geared towards treatment goals. Studies with a wide variety of populations, including elderly individuals in assisted living facilities, people with medical conditions and chronic pain, individuals with developmental and psychiatric disorders, and others have reported positive results.

Frail Elderly Individuals

The reduced independence and increased need for care brought about by aging may be accompanied by a certain amount of depression and social isolation. Dementia may further decrease one's activity and engagement. Living in a residential facility with strangers, many of whom are also depressed, can be a factor as well, and can lead to worries about safety. Studies have found significantly reduced depression in people with dementia in residential care facilities, and decreased anxiety and increased positive emotions and activity levels for participants at an Alzheimer center when they participated in dog-assisted therapy.

As one example, Allesandra Berry and her research team in Rome, Italy found that therapy dogs increased the social behavior of residents and produced significant increases in levels of the hormone cortisol, which is associated with increased activity. Two dogs, a golden retriever and a cocker spaniel, visited the nursing home one morning per week for five months. These researchers concluded that the dogs had an "activational effect" (p. 149) that drew the residents out of their withdrawn, apathetic state.

Post-Operative and Chronic Pain Patients

Chronic pain can be debilitating and difficult to treat. Pain medications may be inadequate or have unwanted side effects, including addiction, and not everyone can tolerate them. Studies found that patients undergoing joint replacement surgery had lower pain levels, less reliance on pain medication and greater post-operative recovery satisfaction when they participated in a dog therapy program. Children receiving treatment at an acute pain care facility also reported decreased pain levels. In one study, children were asked to point to one of six cartoon faces that indicated which of six levels of pain they were experiencing, from no pain/smiling to severe pain/crying. Those who spent time with a therapy dog reported that their pain had been lowered to the same level as if they had taken acetaminophen. Decreases in pain have even been reported by outpatient clinic patients who simply spent time in a waiting area with a therapy dog prior to their appointment.

A study of cancer patients with visiting therapy dogs found that 94% reported improved mood, 91% reported reduced stress, and 88% reported increased relaxation. In another study, breast cancer patients with a therapy dog present during counseling sessions were significantly more likely to (a) look forward to their appointments, (b) feel calmer and more confident during the session, and (c) have improved subsequent communication with health professionals.

Children and Adults with Disabilities

Children with autism spectrum disorders and other developmental disabilities may experience difficulties with social interactions and relationships that interfere with their inclusion into schools and other community settings. Therapy dogs promote increased positive social interaction.

Studies have found that children with autism smile more often and exhibit more positive social behavior in the presence of a dog. Suk-Chung Fung and Alvin Leung, researchers at the Hong Kong Institute of Education and the University of Hong Kong, compared two groups of children with autism participating in play therapy groups; one with a therapy dog and the other with a dog doll. Social behavior was more frequent with the real dog, and the researchers concluded that the dog acted as a "speech elicitor" (p. 253).

Autism researchers Andrea Grigore and Alina Rusu added a therapy dog to another popular intervention for young children with autism, the social story method. They created stories in which a child was shown engaging in two interactions the children were learning: introducing yourself and responding when greeted. Children with autism can sometimes understand interactions like this more easily when they are presented as stories. The group that was read the social story with a dog present, with the dog providing greeting practice by lifting his paw to shake hands, mastered the two skills faster than children using the social story alone.

Children with other disabilities have experienced similar benefits. A research team from the University of California/ Irvine demonstrated that a group of children with attention deficit hyperactivity disorder showed a greater reduction in severity of symptoms than a control group when a dog was a part of their therapy. And researchers affiliated with a child advocacy center in Fort Worth Texas found that children traumatized by sexual abuse showed significant decreases in anxiety, depression, anger, post-traumatic stress disorder, dissociation, and sexual concerns when therapy dogs were used as a component of their treatment, similar to the way Barry Levinson used Jingles as a co-therapist.

The effect of adding a therapy dog to psychotherapy sessions for adults, as Freud did with Jofi, has been explored in two studies.

Researchers in Monterrey Mexico led by Psychologist Monica Gonzelez-Ramirez found that the addition of a dog was beneficial in reducing patient stress, and Melissa Hunt and Rachael Chizkov at the University of Pennsylvania found that having a dog present reduced depressive symptoms in patients experiencing anxiety and trauma disorders.

Therapy dogs have also been found beneficial for veterans with post-traumatic stress disorder. Rick Yount and his colleagues at the Warrior Canine Connection published a study in which they took blood samples from PTSD patients with and without a therapy dog, and measured their levels of oxytocin. Oxytocin, a hormone produced in an area of the brain called the hypothalamus and transmitted through the central nervous system and into the bloodstream, is associated with enhanced feelings of well-being. Patients using a therapy dog had higher levels of oxytocin in their blood.

In another study, adults hospitalized with major depression who were paired with a therapy dog showed reduced anxiety, a symptom that interacts with depression and complicates treatment. And therapy dogs have also been found helpful for increasing the level of social contact and quality of social relationships of individuals with chronic schizophrenia. This is an important finding because social isolation and alienation are common and damaging consequences of this disability, and satisfactory social relationships are an important predictor of successful treatment. Therapy dogs have also helped individuals with schizophrenia to increase their motivation and ability to feel pleasure.

Other Populations

Although the impact of a therapy dog is particularly evident in the case of vulnerable populations and those experiencing difficulties, Psychologist Nancy Gee and her colleagues at the

State University of New York/Fredonia have conducted a series of studies showing that a dog improved learning for typical preschoolers as well. In one experiment she divided children into three groups: One with a real dog named Louie, one with a stuffed dog toy named Kory, and one with a college student intern named Dan. All three groups were told a story about Louie, Kory or Dan taking a train ride to visit their grandmother and bringing ten objects along. The children were shown the objects, then the objects were put away. The children were told that the objects on the train had gotten mixed up so Louie, Kory, or Dan needed help putting the right ones back in their suitcase. The children in each group selected from the ten objects and ten additional items. The children helping Louie more easily remembered which items he was taking and needed less help picking the right ten objects than those helping Dan. The results for Kory were in between.

Dog-assisted therapy has also been found to reduce stress in typical adults, and there is evidence of the value of dogs in the workplace, increasing the job satisfaction of workers.

Service Dog Effectiveness

Service dogs have been used for many years as mobility aids for individuals with vision impairments, and more recently have also been used to assist other individuals. Service dogs live with the individual or their family and accompany the individual throughout their day, whereas therapy dogs are attached to a particular facility or to a contracting organization and people interact with them during scheduled visits.

Service dogs have been found to be especially useful for individuals with developmental disabilities and those on the autism spectrum. Service dogs have a calming influence on children on the autism spectrum and with fetal alcohol syndrome. They have also proven useful for keeping children from getting lost or engaging in impulsive or dangerous behavior. Remaining calm and safe helps these children succeed in community settings and activities. Service dogs also act as social catalysts and conversation starters to help children overcome communication problems and avoid social isolation.

In addition to their effect on children, researchers have found that service dogs can also be valuable for adults on the autism spectrum in employment settings, helping ensure their safety and helping them connect with co-workers. Employees with service dogs also reported an increase in self-assurance that helped them to focus better on their jobs.

Through my employment as a university research professor, I worked with a co-worker, Amy, who brought her dog Judah to work. Amy, a young woman on the autism spectrum, explained that Judah provided her with a feeling of consistency and security that was helpful to her in her work as a research associate and adjunct faculty member. There is also documented evidence that service dogs can be trained to act as an alarm system for people due to their acute sense of smell, alerting individuals with epilepsy to the immanent onset of a seizure or individuals with diabetes to a dangerous rise in their blood glucose levels.

Because service dogs live with the humans they serve, a strong attachment is formed between the dog and the family. Olga Solomon, an expert on linguistics and communication disorders at the University of Southern California, studied the families of two children with autism who used a service dog, in order to understand how the interactions among the child, the dog, and other family members provided support for the child. She recruited families for her study through a parent advocacy organization and visited their homes periodically, collecting videotaped observations and interviews over almost two years. She came to understand what it was about the dog that facilitated a child's success. Most importantly, children who were often confused and disoriented about interpreting complex social behavior felt competent and comfortable interacting with their service dog because the dog's behavior was easy to understand and predict. And verbal sophistication was not required, since dogs primarily communicate through gaze and gestures. This comfort level then generalized to any other situations where the child and the dog accompanied one another.

Children with service dogs consider their dog as one of the most important parts of their lives. Solomon related a touching school essay written by a 13-year old boy with autism about his dog Simon. The assignment was to write an essay called "I like to...".

> I like to play with Simon. I like to Simon a boy. I like to Simon play with ball. I like to Simon swimming pool. I like to walk Simon. I like to black and white dog. He has a tail, ears, nose, mouth, ears and paws. I like to sleep in bed with Simon. I like to play catch the ball with Simon. I like to living a house. I like to go outside. I like to go in the car with Simon. Mom go in the car. Mom buy with dog food. Mom feed Simon. I like to Simon big. I like to brown eyes. I like to black nose (p. 160).

Both therapy and service dogs enjoy and benefit from providing services to humans. Not only do they show no signs of stress, interaction with humans actually reduces stress in dogs. Just as interacting with dogs raises a human's level of oxytocin, a hormone associated with enhanced feelings of well-being, a research team from the University of Sydney, Australia led by Elyssa Payne has shown that dogs shown affection by humans also have increased levels of oxytocin. These researchers concluded that, "The physiological and emotional benefits that ensue from a positive dog-human relationship extend to both members of the dyad" (p. 72).

A noteworthy exception to this finding occurred during the course of a study by Carie Braun and her colleagues at the University of Minnesota with a therapy dog assisting children to deal with chronic pain. The researchers noticed that in situations where children were in severe pain and crying, the dog seemed to take on the pain of the child and become very uncomfortable. The dog's handler noticed this was happening and limited the number of such intense sessions to no more than three per week. The handler also provided massages and other calming measures to the dog after intense sessions.

Explanations of Therapeutic Value

What is it about a dog that has such a profound positive effect on humans in such a wide variety of different contexts? On one level, we can know that something works without knowing how it works. Native Americans knew that chewing the inner bark of a willow tree cured headaches, for example, long before anyone knew that the bark contains the active ingredient in aspirin. And we all are familiar with the pull of gravitation, but Sir Isaac Newton famously said, "I have not as yet been able to discover the reason for these properties of gravity from phenomena" (p. 943), and to this day how gravity works remains a mystery.

But it is important that we seek an explanation for the therapeutic effectiveness of dogs. Part of the initial reluctance to take therapy dogs seriously seems to have been that people could see no way that such effects could be produced, leading them to doubt that they were real. Should anyone doubt that gravity is real, gravity will forcefully remind them, but dogs can't advocate for themselves as readily.

The explanation most often offered for therapeutic effectiveness is that dogs are therapeutic because they are nonjudgmental.

Educational researcher Lori Friesen, for example, stated that "The general assumptions underlying animal-assisted therapy with children are that although therapy dogs are interactive, children seem to perceive them as nonjudgmental participants who are outside of the complications and expectations of human relationships" (p. 261).

But there are difficulties with this explanation. Many other interactive animals are also nonjudgmental and outside the complications of human relationships, but there is far less evidence of therapeutic value for other animals. Cats, horses, other farm animals, rabbits, guinea pigs, gerbils, hamsters, llamas and even birds and fish can be used as therapy animals, but there is almost no evidence of specific benefits using these animals. The benefit of exposure to horses and other farm animals seems to be connected to the context of outdoor field trips and participation in enjoyable activities like horseback riding. There is no evidence that the animals themselves play much of a role.

Information about the therapeutic value of other animals is limited to two types of study. In the first type, other animals are used along with dogs, such as dogs and cats, or dogs, cats and rabbits. The obvious problem here is that we have no way of knowing which animal had which effect. If the effect was positive, most or all of it may have been due to the dogs. In the second type of study, the effect of a dog is compared with the effect of another animal. But only one study of this type has been published. The blood pressure of college students was measured after handling a dog or a cat. Both animals reduced blood pressure, but only slightly, with no difference between the two animals. Not much can be concluded from this one study.

Another difficulty with the nonjudgmental explanation is the fact that dogs are not entirely nonjudgmental of humans. (This is even more true for cats, who would probably be offended if anyone suggested that they are nonjudgmental.) Dogs are quick to indicate their approval of a positive action, whereas in order to be truly nonjudgmental one has to be consistent – rendering neither positive nor negative judgments. And many dogs are also not shy about communicating the occasional negative judgment in response to humans being late in serving a meal or taking them outside, young children being too bouncy or too loud, and other behaviors that bother or seem out of line to them.

A closely related explanation also frequently offered is that dogs provide humans with unconditional love and acceptance. Mary Burch offers this explanation in her book *Wanted: Animal Volunteers*. But this explanation is also too simplistic. Dogs have friends and enemies. There are people they distrust. A dog may indicate dislike of a particular person, or a whole category of people, or, as dog cognition experts Brian Hare and Vanessa Woods pointed out, will sometimes turn against a person they formerly liked.

One might argue that therapy dogs are specially trained for their work, and thus are more accepting and less judgmental than just any dog. But it is difficult to understand how such behavior could be taught to a dog. The concept "nonjudgmental," and the companion term "unconditional acceptance," were introduced in the 1940s by counseling and psychotherapy theorists, particularly Carl Rogers. In his book *Client-Centered Therapy* Rogers recommended that counselors remain nonjudgmental and communicate "the counselor's acceptance of the client as a person who is competent to direct himself" (p. 24). This counseling attitude was part of a humanistic psychology movement which Rogers helped pioneer. Rogers stressed that it is a mistake to view being accepting and nonjudgmental as passive, because "a laissez faire attitude does not in any way indicate to the client that he is regarded as a person of worth" (p. 27). Being nonjudgmental is not the kind of behavior that can be taught to a dog.

In his later book *On Becoming a Person*, an expanded and updated formulation of client-centered therapy, Rogers introduced the term "unconditional positive regard" as one of the attitudes he believed promoted therapeutic progress. In this work he argued even more forcefully against a passive approach. Communicating unconditional acceptance requires active listening techniques. In sessions with clients, counselors and therapists use encouragers like "I see" or "go on" at appropriate points, and paraphrase client statements to check comprehension. Unconditional acceptance also includes helping the client identify the feelings behind a statement, and may include some self-disclosure by the counselor. Several years of post-graduate and clinical training are required before these skills can be used properly. This level of complexity is clearly out of reach for dogs.

On Becoming a Person has been a widely influential work that has never gone out of print, and several concepts, "nonjudgmental" and "unconditional positive regard" among them, have entered the mainstream of our culture and are now used in a variety of ways to mean a variety of things. As explanations for the therapeutic effect of dogs, these concepts are too superficial. If there is a kernel of truth in such explanations, it is a kernel that needs much more expansion. We must dig deeper to find the explanation we are seeking.

Courtney Zents, Amy Fisk and Chris Lauback studied the impact of dogs in two public schools in western New York. The dogs spent their days interacting with students at each school in an attempt to increase student attendance and motivation. Through interviews with faculty and students these researchers discovered five factors that they believed characterized the dogs' impact. One, which they called unconditional love, is virtually the same as unconditional acceptance, which we have seen may contain a kernel of truth but is too simplistic as it stands. The other four factors – Feeling Understood, Lifting Spirits, Reciprocity and

Companionship, and a Calming Effect – may help expand and clarify the explanation of therapeutic value.

Feeling Understood

What is it that we feel that dogs understand about us? If dogs entertain concepts in their minds, they are rudimentary ones. Dogs certainly do not understand things in anywhere near the way humans do. Yet there is something important that people feel and that they express as being understood, albeit from the perspective of another species, that seems particularly meaningful. The novelist Thomas Mann commented about the ability of his dog Bashan to understand him: "He sees what my intentions are. My clothes betray these to him, the cane that I carry, also my attitude and expression, the cool and preoccupied look I give him, or the irritation and challenge in my eyes. He understands" (quoted in Brottman, p. 45). Dogs certainly understand things like this. They are acutely sensitive to our actions and our moods, in part because they are a highly social species, as we are, and the social context is important to them, as it is to us. They attend to the details of social situations and respond in ways that show that they care about being a good companion and a good family member. This is something hardly any other animal does.

Lifting Spirits

Whatever it is that dogs understand about us they seem to mostly find pleasant, even delightful. And they have no self-consciousness about showing affection or acting silly. That cannot help but lift our spirits. The way they live in the present moment and throw themselves wholeheartedly into any activity can seem refreshing and even in some ways instructive for our human lives. Author James Thurber once remarked that people long to be as happy and carefree as a dog.

Reciprocity and Companionship

Dogs observe us closely and resonate with the flow of our actions and feelings. The 19th century composer Richard Wagner had a dog named Peps – an English toy or Cavalier King Charles spaniel – who rested on a cushion next to the piano while Wagner composed music. At some point Wagner became aware that Peps responded to the emotional tone his compositions produced. The responses were not random, they seemed to vary with differences in the key of the music. The key of Eb minor was accompanied by a calm tail wag. When the key changed to E major, Peps raised his head in an excited manner.

In his opera *Lohengrin* Wagner used hints supplied in this way by Peps to give each main character his or her own key. For example, passages featuring Lohengrin, the hero, were in A major. Those featuring Ortrud, the villain, were in F# minor. Wagner informally referred to Peps as the coauthor of *Lohengrin*. In this and his subsequent works, frequent key changes became a signature feature of Wagner's compositions, and this innovation had a lasting influence on the history of music.

A relationship with a dog can even help us respond better to the emotions of other people. A study by Brigit Stetina and her colleagues at the University of Vienna showed that both children and adults were able to identify emotions in people faster and more accurately after observing those emotions in dogs. We apparently use human-dog interactions, at least some of the time, to help us understand our human-human interactions.

Calming Effect

An important part of a dog's responsiveness is that they like to be physically close and feel the touch of their bodies against ours. Touch has a calming effect, and we never question motives or look for complex interpretations when a dog snuggles up to us.

In 1961, in the midst of the Cuban missile crisis, President Kennedy's national security team was gathered in the Oval Office. Messages were being sent back and forth between the U.S. and the Soviet Union, and options were being considered. As the crisis intensified, the room became extraordinarily tense. The world was on the brink of nuclear war. At that point President Kennedy asked for his terrier Charlie to be brought to him. Charlie lept into Kennedy's lap as he continued to listen to the discussion while petting his dog. After a while, Kennedy seemed to visibly relax. He handed Charlie back to the White House kennel keeper and announced, "OK, now its time to make some decisions" (quoted in Coren, 2002, p. 266). Kennedy's calm responses are often credited with resolving the crisis.

It is unreasonable to suggest that this sort of calming effect can be explained simply by saying that Charlie was nonjudgmental and accepting. Clearly, President Kennedy and Charlie had a deep bond with one another. Charlie knew what his friend needed from him in that moment, and no doubt the physical contact between the two of them was an important part of their relationship. The calming effect of dogs on humans is both profound and mysterious.

Sigmund Freud speculated in his letters about what it was about dogs that had the impact he observed with Jofi during psychoanalysis sessions. His correspondence about dogs was primarily with Marie Bonaparte, with whom he shared a love of dogs. It was Marie Bonaparte, granddaughter of Napoleon's brother, who paid ransom to Nazi officials to allow the Freud family to emigrate from Austria to England in 1938 rather than being sent to a concentration camp. In his letters to her, Freud speculated that the dog gave his patients a sense of safety and a feeling of reassurance. In one letter (#228), he wrote that dogs offer "affection without ambivalence, the simplicity of life free from the almost unbearable conflicts of civilization, the beauty of an existence complete in itself. And yet there is the feeling of an intimate affinity, of an undeniable solidarity."

The simplicity of our relationship with dogs seems to provide a welcome contrast to the complexity of the rest of our lives. Olga Solomon found that children having difficulty with social relationships could feel successful with a service dog because a dog's behavior is not difficult to understand. This appreciation of simplicity, as a welcome respite from the bewildering confusion of human relationships, is by no means confined to children or to people with disabilities. Frederick the Great of Prussia is said to have remarked "The more I deal with people, the more I like my dog" (quoted in Coren, 2002, p. 65).

But why would a patient of Freud's talking with him in his office feel safer and more peaceful with Jofi around? Why would the children Barry Levinson was treating for emotional disturbance make more progress when Jingles was present? We have still not fully answered these questions.

The way the presence of a dog can make us feel more relaxed and secure must have something to do with a uniquely deep and enduring bond that our two species have formed with one another. British biologist Peter Smith, interviewed for BBC News, reminds us that a "deep, deep connection has existed between man and wolves – now dogs – for many tens of thousands of years, and that is why we love dogs so much. They are part of our own evolution into a modern society."

It might not be too far off the mark to say that our bond with dogs completes us in some way. Roman author Flavius Arrian wrote a book called *Cynegeticus* (hunting with dogs) in about the year 110. After being lost for many centuries, the book was rediscovered, translated from Latin and published in English in 1831 by William Dansey. Dansey's introduction to Arrian's book seems to hint in this direction: "Man, by cooperating with such animals, employs both his and their faculties on the purposes for which they were partially designed, tending thereby to complete the bounteous scheme of Providence, the happiness and well-being of all its creatures" (p. 18).

What happened over tens of thousands of years that made dogs who they are, us who we are, and the bond between us so powerful?

2

Wise Humans

To understand our bond with dogs we need to start at the beginning. Our species of primate evolved in Africa from earlier species of the genus *homo* between 200,000 – 100,000 years ago. The wide time range reflects in part the fact that a new species develops in tiny increments over a great many generations, with no clear line separating the new from the old. It also reflects the fact that archaeological evidence tends to be inconclusive. Only a small subset of past objects remains, and archaeological finds are largely accidental and piecemeal. Most evidence of early humans has disappeared or has not been found. In addition, because ground is disturbed over time and objects are carried from place to place by animals, and so forth, dating objects found in the field involves a certain amount of interpretation. And methods of dating themselves have some wiggle room and are periodically improved, requiring re-calculation of the age of objects. So dates long ago must always be understood as best guesses made at a particular point in time.

As we became a distinct species, we developed thinner bones, a smaller overall size, smaller teeth with a more rounded bite, and a shortened face, with a chin. The size of our cranium became larger in relation to our overall size. Our adult human skeletal structure actually became more physically similar to juveniles of the species we evolved from. This is known as paedomorphosis, and when characteristics involving soft tissues and behavior are considered in addition to skeletal structure, the process is called neoteny. Paedomorphosis and neoteny may seem like a backwards step rather than an advance, but they are not. Slowing down the rate at which some parts of the biological system develop is an efficient way for an emerging new species to adapt to its environment.

A good way to think about our development as a species is that just about everything else was sacrificed so that we could have the largest possible cognitive capacity. To increase the size of our brain that deals with higher cognitive functions in proportion to our overall size, we had to be born at a less developed stage, before a baby's head became too big for safe delivery. Thus, humans bear children with very little hair and with brains that start out relatively undeveloped and grow larger and better organized over several years. And we lack most of the instinctive behaviors that other animals possess, so instead of being wired for specialized built-in behaviors, our brains are built primarily for maximum general-purpose cognitive power.

As we evolved, our eyes also changed in a way that allows the whites (the sclera) to show around the pupils. Modern humans are unique among primates in having white eyeballs around the pupils as well as eyelids that expose part of the eyeball. Having pupils that stand out against a white background allows other people to see where we are looking, and allows us to see where they are looking. This change allowed us to take on tasks involving complex social interactions.

The human face changed in other ways as well. Our faces became flatter, our tongues moved deeper into the throat, and we developed a concave roof of the mouth. These changes gave us good binocular vision and made articulate speech easier, further facilitating complex social interaction. But they had a negative side effect: They reduced the acuteness of our sense of smell.

Before our species appeared on the scene, the brains of our ancestors had been getting progressively larger and their cognitive ability had been increasing. Earlier species of the genus *homo* mastered the use of fire and the cooking of food, had adopted an upright posture and had begun living in open grasslands rather than in forests. This allowed them to scan the surrounding landscape and find animals to hunt. Humans probably hunted in groups, since a coordinated group of hunters is more efficient than a solitary individual. Group hunting required complex social interactions, and these interactions, in turn, helped drive further brain development.

The animals we preyed upon were killed at close range with simple hand-axes. Open grassland provided humans with sufficient protein-rich meat to fuel large brains. But living in the open also made our ancestors more of a target for large nocturnal predators such as the big cats.

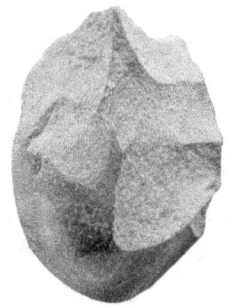 

2. Early Stone Hand-Axes

The Emergence of Wise Humans

Increasing cognitive capacity eventually led to the emergence of *homo sapiens* – "wise humans" – as a new species. The skulls of the earliest *homo sapiens* are indistinguishable from those of humans today, so we assume that their brain size and components were the same, and they had the same cognitive capacity we have.

Perhaps the most important indicator archaeologists use to mark the emergence of our ancestors as a new species is that between 200,000 and 100,000 years ago we began to carefully and ritualistically bury our dead. The first evidence of such burials came from caves in a region of present day Israel called Skhul, on the slopes of Mount Carmel, and Qafzeh, in Galilee. Qafez is a cave complex on a hillside just southeast of Nazareth. It happens to be the hill mentioned in the New Testament *Bible* (Luke 4:29) as the place where the people of Nazareth almost threw Jesus off a cliff because they were upset that the local carpenter's son had the audacity to lecture them on how to live.

Ritualistic burial distinguishes *homo sapiens* from earlier species of the genus *homo* and from all other animals. It implies an awareness of death most likely made possible by our highly developed cognitive capacity. Some other animals mourn dead friends and relatives, but carefully organized burial rituals indicate a deeper level of awareness. They suggest that death was a significant event for a social group. They are evidence of an awareness that death was something that regularly happened to group members.

Group customs in connection with funerals and burial, and the transmission of those customs from one generation to another, also implies some form of communication, so ritualistic burial is considered indirect evidence that "wise humans" had advanced to the point of having symbolic language. It is impossible to exaggerate the importance of this invention. Earlier species of the genus *homo* may have had rudimentary forms of language, as do some other animals, but fully symbolic language – made up of sounds that are assigned specific meanings that refer to objects, actions, and so on, plus a grammar or syntax of rules for sequencing sounds to form statements or questions and distinguish between things like singular or plural and past, present or future – this was the singular achievement of *homo sapiens*. Anthropologist Ian Tattersall, curator emeritus of the

American Museum of Natural History, has called the changeover from a non-symbolic, nonlinguistic species to a symbolic, linguistic one the most significant cognitive transformation that has ever happened to any organism.

Another important finding has been that some ritualistic burials contained funeral objects such as colored shells and beads deliberately placed on or next to the person being buried. Colored beads have been found in today's Israel and in Algeria dated to 100,000 years ago, and colored, perforated shells have been found deliberately buried with skeletons at Blombos Cave, a site in South Africa on the shoreline of the Indian Ocean, dated to about 75,000 years ago.

Perforating and adding bright color to shells and beads did not serve any obvious survival function, so these objects are thought to be decorative, indicating both an appreciation of beauty and the fact that humans had advanced to the point where they could devote time to non-survival-related tasks. These objects may have had cultural meaning as well. For example, they may have been worn as markers of group affiliation or of age or social status, providing further evidence of the ability to think symbolically and maintain complex social structures. Burying someone wearing the necklace they wore in life indicated that humans understood that the meaning of the object was connected with that person, and perhaps that the person's spirit might appreciate having it in an afterlife.

The care with which humans paid attention to death indicates something else besides. It shows that the members of this new species had come to the realization not just that someone they knew had died, but that each of them was also going to die.

David Hagner, Ph.D.

The Price of Wisdom

As a species evolves, a new trait offers a net fitness advantage, but there may also be a cost involved. Our increased cognitive capacity gave humans an enormous survival advantage, but it also had noteworthy side effects, generating difficulties that no other animal has had to face.

We have noted that large brains gave humans a difficult and risky childbirth, and that changes to our faces allowing easier communication reduced our sense of smell. Other difficulties confronted us as well. First, we had to learn to create and to obey demanding social rules in order live in ordered societies. Second, we had to deal with the psychological complications that go along with increased cognitive capacity. And third, we had to adapt to the increased need for sleep that increased cognitive complexity requires.

Social Complexity and Rules

The amount and complexity of social cooperation required of us is extraordinary. This partly results from the fact that being born at a less developed stage requires an extended period of childhood. Human children remain largely helpless and dependent on adults for many years, far longer than any other animal. Childrearing requires group cooperation and some sort of division of labor, so that some people mind the children while others hunt, find firewood, fashion tools, and so on. Social rules had to be developed to govern this effort. Complex communication is also required to educate children whose brains are expanding and consolidating. Lacking most instinctive behavior, young children had to be kept safe and taught the rules for social behavior, while older children needed to be mentored step by step in the knowledge and skill required to participate in adult tasks. Children also had to learn to communicate with and solicit help from numerous others.

The threat of predation from large nocturnal animals probably also drove humans to live and sleep in larger groups, to better defend themselves. Primates living in the wild today experience less predation the larger the group size. There is strength in numbers but complexity as well. Dealing with social groups is far more challenging than dealing with the physical world. Neuroscientist Michael Gazzaniga has called the mental effort needed to negotiate large numbers of social interactions the "cost of grouping" (p. 71). As the size of a group increases, the number of interactions each human has to keep track of increases exponentially. A little math will show why this is. If you are a member of a group of eight people, you need to be aware of 28 different relationships (7 factorial: $7 + 6 + 5 + 4 + 3 + 2 + 1$). But if the group size doubles, you now have to keep track of 120 relationships (15 factorial), more than four times as many.

We don't know the actual size of early human groups. Perhaps a fair estimate can be drawn from accounts of societies in historic times living in somewhat similar circumstances. Eugene Delessert, a French explorer who visited the aboriginal people in Australia in the mid-19th century, reported that a group living together was composed of 20 to 25 individuals.

Increases in social complexity eventually led to the development of orderly rules for conduct that group members were expected to obey and that were taught to young people. Rules were needed to govern the distribution of tasks among members and how food from hunting and gathering expeditions was to be allocated. General interaction rules like telling the truth, keeping promises, asking first before taking something, and so on, had to be formalized. Over time, rules for cooperative group behavior became ingrained in us as a set of reactions and judgments that we now associate with morality and justice. *Homo sapiens* is a moral species.

Moral judgments seem to be hard-wired into the prefrontal cortex region of the human brain. Evidence for this can be gleaned from decision-making studies of individuals with traumatic injury to this region of the brain. In one study, a group of such individuals and a nondisabled control group were given moral dilemmas to solve like this one:

> You are walking down the street when you see a wallet on the ground. You open it and find it contains cash and the address of the owner. By the number of credit cards and other documents you realize that the owner of the wallet is probably rich, while you, on the other hand, could really use more money. Would you keep the money? (Martins, et al., p. 482).

A higher proportion of individuals with traumatic brain injury reported that they would resolve the dilemma by keeping the cash, indicating impaired moral judgment.

Psychological Stress

The 19th century historian Daniel Tuke held the mistaken view that early humans were immune from psychological disturbance because their lives were so simple. "From intellectual strain and its concomitants, the man of the Stone Age was certainly free. Rather from club-blows in battle was his brain likely to suffer (p. 12)." But the ability to manipulate abstract concepts, imagine things that are physically impossible, review the past and speculate about the future, consider multiple scenarios, weave bits of information into theories, and so on, introduces challenging psychological complications. Biologists Ajit Varky and Danny Brower pointed out that this type of analysis can easily lead to confusion and mental dysfunction. So one of the costs that goes along with having a large prefrontal cortex is the potential for becoming confused or obsessed by the complexity of thoughts our minds can generate.

The imposition of moral rules created additional difficulties, as humans were required to learn to restrain their impulses, delay gratification, wait for their turn, and develop willpower. For the first time, our ancestors had to make compromises, resolve moral dilemmas, and cope with such emotions as guilt about transgressions and anxiety about being reprimanded. At some point, behaviors like apologizing, repairing hurt feelings and asking for forgiveness became critical necessities. Eventually, second-order rules – rules about the rules – were imposed for things like acknowledging obedience, resolving disagreements, and punishing rule-breakers.

For children, remaining for years in a relatively dependent state introduced additional psychological stresses. A child is aware of being relatively small and weak, with few defenses against what appears as a massively confusing and dangerous world. Events adults take for granted, like thunder and lightning, are often frightening. Developing brains tend to generate imaginary and fanciful explanations for things that seem incomprehensible. Most children are bothered by nightmares. And they have to face the consequences of making mistakes, including perhaps being punished by those they depend on. A certain amount of anxiety has always been part of the cost of developing into an adult human. This is supported by contemporary child development studies showing that more fearful children show greater moral understanding.

The awareness of death that accompanied our development into modern humans introduced concerns of its own. Our ancestors no doubt wondered what happened to a person's spirit – the person "inside" the body – after they died, and what might happen to their own spirit one day. Varky and Brower theorized that the recognition of mortality was frightening to our ancestors. There has always been a need for humans to deal with all of these types of psychological stress and to treat psychological disturbance.

Increased Sleep Requirements

One of the fundamental problems we wise humans have to face in dealing with cognitive complexity is how to deal with the prodigious amount of information we are presented with each day. For information to be of use, it must be sorted according to its importance and organized. We must identify patterns, track them over time, and apply the right information at the right time to make decisions.

To handle these tasks effectively, we require periods of time devoted to background processing, without exposure to new sensory information. This is what sleep provides. Apparently all animals sleep, but different animals have different sleep patterns. Many can doze lightly, or even sleep with half their brain at a time. This doesn't work for humans. As one of the costs of our expanded cognitive capacity, we need a substantial daily period of deep sleep to function at our best. Inadequate sleep has serious negative effects on our cognitive functioning. Even sleep disruptions in children as young as one year old have been linked to later disturbances in cognitive functioning.

For early humans, adequate sleep was by no means guaranteed. Sleeping out in the open made us sitting ducks for predators. There was a particularly serious danger that infants and children would be snatched away. In addition, there were times when the most physically strong members of a group were away on hunting expeditions. Large cats such as tigers and leopards were an especially serious threat since they hunt at night, have excellent nocturnal vision, and are extremely stealthy. To illustrate the seriousness of this threat, there is a recorded case in India in modern times of a baby being taken from the breast of a sleeping mother by a leopard without the mother waking up.

We are diurnal animals with poor eyesight after dark and no other senses acute enough to compensate. Facial changes allowing articulate speech weakened our sense of smell. How did we protect ourselves? Campfires helped keep predators at bay, but cooking meat also attracted all the meat-loving animals in the neighborhood. We lived in caves when available, but caves only offer partial protection, and the supply of ideal cave sites was finite, with humans having to compete with other animals such as bears for available sites.

No doubt humans took turns standing watch at night. But that in itself creates some level of sleep deprivation. So these were imperfect responses to a serious problem. The archaeological record shows many early human bones that had been chewed by predators. It is a good bet that our ancestors had difficulty sleeping as deeply or as securely as they needed to on a consistent basis.

Wallace's Conundrum

Despite these difficulties, the expanded cognitive ability of our ancestors conferred a net advantage in adapting to our environment. Earlier species of the genus *homo* had mastered the technology for using fire and cooking meat and for hunting with hand-axes, but about 400,000 years ago some groups invented something new: Spears and spear-points. Spears allowed them to kill prey animals from farther away than hand-axes, making hunting more effective and less dangerous.

This is pretty much the same level of technology used by *homo sapiens* during what is called the early or lower paleolithic (old stone age) period, ranging from the time we emerged as a species, 200,000 – 100,000 years ago until about 60,000 years ago. The lives of these ancestors of ours were extraordinarily simple. They wore skins when the weather was cold and lived in caves or temporary shelters of branches or hides. But even though human brains had evolved to the same size as ours today, and most likely all of our modern human mental abilities were fully established, advances in technology were few and far between. The development of technology did not pick up noticeably as we became wise humans. This has seemed counter-intuitive to anthropologists.

During the middle paleolithic period, beginning about 60,000 years ago, groups of *homo sapiens* migrated from Africa into Eurasia, beginning a journey that eventually took us to every corner of the earth. A few biological adjustments were made along the way, such as lighter skin color for those who migrated farther from the equator. As we explored Eurasia we encountered other species already well adapted to the climate, food supply and other conditions there. These included other species of the genus *homo* who had ventured out of Africa earlier: Neanderthals (also spelled Neandertals) in Europe, and a related species in Asia called Denisovans. DNA analysis shows that a small amount of interbreeding took place between our species and these other groups, but more archaeological work will be needed before we have a clearer understanding of how they might have interacted.

There were also new prey animals to be hunted and competition from new predators, many much larger and fiercer than those in Eurasia during historic times. And we crossed paths with another Eurasian inhabitant who was also an efficient predator and also hunted in groups and was after the same prey: The wolf.

During the middle paleolithic period, between about 60,000 – 40,000 years ago, a few new technologies appear in the archaeological record. A technique for making thinner spear-points was introduced, allowing thin slightly concave stone points to be manufactured by knocking flakes from a prepared core. This new blade-flaking method allowed a large number of spear-points to be produced quickly and efficiently once the right kind of rock was obtained. Humans also developed primitive forms of pottery during middle paleolithic times and created the first primitive oil lamps – small stone dishes or seashells filled with moss soaked in animal fat.

3. Blade-Flaked Stone Point

But advances in technology remained scattered and largely unremarkable. Wise humans possessed super-computing brains with a level of cognitive power that seems out of proportion to their relatively simple lifestyles. Alfred Russell Wallace, who independently and almost simultaneously with Charles Darwin formulated the theory of evolution – with Darwin getting the credit because he published it first – remarked how odd it was that humans had mental abilities at least 100,000 years ago that they would not use until much later. In Wallace's own words,

> ...the capacity to form ideal conceptions of space and time, of eternity and infinity – the capacity for intense artistic feelings of pleasure, in form, colour, and composition – and for those abstract notions of form and number which render geometry and arithmetic possible. How were any of these faculties first developed, when they could have been of no possible use to man in his early stages of barbarism? (pp. 351-352.)

This discrepancy became known as "Wallace's Conundrum". Something seemed to be holding us back from the full use of our immense cognitive capacity.

Wallace, and others since his time, considered this a difficulty for the theory of evolution by natural selection because it seemed to suggest that nature was planning ahead for the distant future. Natural selection can only favor traits currently adaptive, not those that will come in handy in the future. Wallace simply noted this difficulty as something curious and worth further investigation. But in fact, it isn't a difficulty at all for the theory. The human brain evolved supercomputing powers that conferred an immediate adaptive advantage over simpler brains. But these same brains also contained, in latent or dormant form, the capacity to do many other things as well. No future planning was involved. It just so happened that in the case of *homo sapiens,* instead of specific structures like a shell or camouflage color, or specific instincts such as burrowing or courtship dances, natural selection embedded within our species a general-purpose computing ability that allowed us to design an unlimited number of new adaptations as needed. But there seemed to be a long period of delay before we developed very many of these. Wallace's Conundrum was a puzzle for anthropologists.

Eventually, though, humans broke through this barrier and technological developments began to flourish. And when it happened, the transition was striking and rapid.

3

All Out Paleo

As humans embarked on the late or upper paleolithic period, we took such a quantum leap in creativity and invention that this period has also been called the "creative explosion" and the "human revolution". Historians James McClellan and Harold Dorn consider this to be a "cultural discontinuity" (p. 9) because the developments during that period were so strikingly different from what came before.

Most anthropologists date the beginning of the late paleolithic advance at 40,000 - 35,000 years ago. But as with almost everything in archaeology, the dates are controversial. Penn State anthropologist Pat Shipman has set a slightly earlier time frame, from 45,000 and 35,000 years ago, for the beginning of changes "so extraordinary that they indicate a huge shift" (p. 156). And Chris Stringer, a British anthropologist with London's Natural History Museum, dated the beginning of the advance even earlier, from about 50,000 years ago, so long ago that it would encompass innovations we have placed within the middle paleolithic period.

But there is one thing almost everyone agrees on. The late paleolithic advance was not a single sudden burst but a staggered process that gradually become more widespread. In the beginning, at least, the advance was piecemeal. Innovations occurred in different places at different times, and some discoveries may even have been made and then lost or abandoned and later rediscovered. The technique for making a particular type of tool, for example, might have only been known by a few people, and those individuals may have died without being able to pass down their technique to the next generation. Life was precarious in those days. Whole human groups may have been wiped out by disease or disasters, and along with them whatever technology they had developed.

Late Paleolithic Advances

Nevertheless, something remarkable undoubtedly happened and then expanded and solidified as the late paleolithic period got underway. After a very long period of very slow progress, extraordinary developments took place in a comparatively short period of time. A look at these developments will help us appreciate their importance.

Substantial Dwellings

Humans began building sturdy huts and tents during the upper paleolithic period that provided better protection against the elements and can be considered the first real dwellings. One interesting type of hut was made by layering wooly mammoth hides over an igloo-shaped frame created from this gigantic creature's ribs and other bones. Hunters who brought down a woolly mammoth were rewarded with both food and shelter.

These and other types of dwellings also became organized during the late paleolithic period into settlement complexes that contained butchering areas, food storage pits, drying racks for food preservation, hearths, and tool-making areas as well as dwellings. Such settlement complexes point to an expansion of the size of human groups living together, and probably also to the beginnings of specialized occupations.

Finer Stone Tools

A stone-working technique called pressure-flaking came to replace the blade-flaking technique during the late paleolithic period and led to the manufacture of superior hunting and butchering tools. In pressure-flaking, a spear-point or knife was produced by hammering on a tool such as the tip of a deer antler that functioned like a chisel, rather than directly on a stone core. This produced a thinner, more even blade that could be fashioned into a variety of desired tool shapes fairly easily. Pressure-flaking could also retouch or sharpen a tool to give it a longer life.

New Hunting Equipment

While spears were a big improvement over hand-axes for bringing down prey, their range was still fairly limited. A late paleolithic invention called the atlatl greatly expanded the range and power of a spear. The atlatl is a flat stick with a hook in the back that fits into a socket or groove at the base of a spear. When a spear is inserted, the atlatl acts as a sort of catapult that multiplies the force, distance, and accuracy of the spear. A spear thrown with an atlatl can travel five times the distance of a hand-held spear at over 90 miles per hour. The word "atlatl" comes to us from the Aztecs, who used this weapon in the 16th century to fight the Spanish invaders of the New World. Spanish soldiers were surprised to find that spears thrown from an atlatl had enough force to pierce their metal body armor.

4. Atlatl Throwers

Another game-changing weapon was the bow and arrow. Stone points believed to be arrowheads have been found dated to about 30,000 years ago in today's Spain, which would place it among the late paleolithic advances. But similar small stone points dated to 70,000 years ago have been found in today's South Africa. Since the wooden bows and arrows themselves are long gone, and stone points almost identical to arrowheads were probably used earlier for darts, dating the origin of the bow and arrow is especially difficult.

Whether invented during the middle or the late paleolithic period, what makes the bow and arrow particularly fascinating is that the technology for producing bows, as difficult as that was to invent, was the easy part. The hard part is that arrows don't fly straight unless pieces of bird feathers called "fletchings" are attached to the back. The physics involved is fairly complex, and early humans would have had nothing to go on in figuring this out other than trial and error or perhaps observing birds in flight.

Pottery

Unfired clay was used during the middle paleolithic period to line baskets, creating a simple pot that could carry liquids, but these were not durable containers. The first true pottery dates from the late paleolithic period, when a technique called pit firing was developed. Kilns were not invented until later, but pots or other clay objects such as beads and figurines were placed in a simple pit and then covered by a fire until they hardened into durable ceramic objects. At an archaeological site in the Czech Republic, 25,000-year-old figurines of fired clay have been unearthed that seem to have been used in rituals or for spiritual healing. The earliest pottery so far found is from the Xianrendong Cave ("Cave of the Immortals") in southeastern China, dated to about 20,000 years ago.

Processing and Cooking Grain

Some people today whose diet contains little or no grain or cereal products call this a "paleo diet," because they believe that paleolithic people did not eat these foods. But paleolithic people could not afford to be picky. Their diet plan was simple: Eat anything edible. Late paleolithic grinding and pounding stones have been found that were used for making a coarse flour out of grains and nuts. One such stone was used about 32,000 years ago in a cave called the Grotto Paglicci in southern Italy, across from Naples on Italy's eastern coast. Archaeologists from the University of Florence found a sandstone pestle at this site with residue from ground acorns, wild oats and an ancient grain similar to millet. These grains and nuts would have been foraged from naturally growing grasses and trees. Analysis of the residue showed that they had been heat-dried, possibly to make grinding easier. This first flour was probably mixed with water and then baked into some sort of unleavened flatbread.

Fiber Material

Wild flax fibers from 34,000-year-old thread or twine have been found at a cave site in the Republic of Georgia. Some of these fibers appear to have been dyed black, gray, and turquoise. The fibers were twisted, suggesting that they had been used to make thread, string, or rope. Thread could have also been used to sew leather pieces together. Thicker twine or rope could have been used to tie logs together or to make nets.

In addition to plant fibers, the remains of knotted and spun mountain goat hairs, a primitive form of wool, have been dated to about 32,000 years ago. Pieces of clay have been preserved that contain the impressions of fiber weaving from 27,000 - 25,000 years ago. And residues of animal skin pants, shirts, and shoes have been found in a 22,000-year-old grave in Russia near Moscow.

Bone Tools

Long thin knives, awls for punching holes in leather, needles with "eyes", clothing fasteners, fish hooks and harpoons with barbs, and many other useful implements were fashioned from bone for the first time during the late paleolithic period. These tools were used in hunting and fishing and in the manufacture of clothing, shoes and tents.

5. Late Paleolithic Bone Tools

Toolmaking Tools and Compound Tools

The late paleolithic period saw the first abundant evidence of tools for making other tools. We have noted that antler tips were used for pressure-flaking. Stone chisels were also used to make and shape other implements out of bone, antler, and ivory. Additional tools for working on other implements included punches and spear shaft straighteners.

Another important development was the use of compound tools, such as detachable spear foreshafts. If one part broke, the tool could be repaired rather than replacing the entire tool.

Artwork

Carved figurines were produced beginning about 32,000 years ago, including the female statuettes often called "Venus figurines" (incorrectly, though, because paleolithic people never heard of Venus). These are sculptures of usually pregnant nude women with large buttocks and breasts. Because of the exaggerated sexual characteristics, they are thought to be ritual objects symbolizing female fertility.

6. Venus Figurine

Late paleolithic humans also left numerous paintings on the walls of caves. Over 150 European caves have been found with paintings on their walls, primarily in today's Southwest France and Northern Spain. Most of the paintings, such as the charcoal drawings of bison and rhinoceroses in the Chauvet cave in France, date from about 32,000 years ago. But red paintings outlining human hands have been discovered in the northern Spanish cave of El Castillo that were made about 40,000 years ago, at the dawn of the late paleolithic period.

The majority of cave paintings depict remarkably realistic prey animals. Most of this art was made deep inside caves, in hard-to-get-to dark areas. Such areas were very likely sacred, used for magical or religious functions. Many of them also have interesting acoustic qualities, suggesting that they may have been used for ceremonies accompanied by music or rhythmic chanting, to induce trance-like states or call upon animal or ancestral spirits. Footprints of adults and children found near some of the paintings has suggested a connection with initiation ceremonies from childhood to adulthood.

Music Instruments

Bird-bone flutes have been found in today's Germany and France, ranging from 35,000 – 20,000 years ago. These instruments are fairly sophisticated, with holes beveled for a tight fingertip seal to allow clear notes to be produced.

Other instruments include drumsticks and bull roarers – noise makers consisting of a flat oval slab of rock, bone, or wood with a hole in one end through which a string is attached. When it is whirled rapidly by the string, a noise is produced. A bull roarer a few inches in length produces a humming sound, but some were several feet in length and produced a loud roaring sound.

Astronomical Observations

Engraved fragments of reindeer and mammoth bones have been found dating to as early as 25,000 years ago with engraved sequences of circles and crescent shapes. They are believed to have been an early form of lunar calendar, recording the phases of the moon. A calendar of this kind may have aided in keeping track of seasonally available foods and migrating herds.

Data Storage

Sequential markings on bones have been found from late paleolithic times that appear to record quantities of some kind, perhaps the number of prey killed or number of people at a ceremony. These have been called the first external memory storage systems, and they were a primitive precursor of writing.

Longer Lifetimes

Better and safer hunting tools and better care of sick and injured members of the group led to a lengthening of the average human lifespan during the late paleolithic period from about 30 to 40 years. While short by our standards, these longer lifespans brought numerous advantages. They expanded the size of human groups. They allowed more time for individuals to accumulate knowledge, become better skilled, and teach others. Longer lifetimes also meant that, for the first time, a sizeable percentage of humans had living grandparents. Grandparents helped provide care and training for children, shared their wisdom, and passed along the stories and traditions that helped build cohesive societies.

It is easy to imagine grandparents long ago being faced with the same questions they hear from children today: "Did the deer we are eating have a mommy?" "Why isn't Grandpa coming back any more?" "Are monsters real?" "Why do people do mean things?" The answers to such questions, and the accompanying stories about those who had lived earlier, developed into the folklore and myths that came to define the culture of the group.

Long Distance Trade

Stone, shell, and other raw materials have been found far from their sources during the late paleolithic period. For example, spear-points have been found that were fashioned from flint brought there from more than 80 miles away, and shells have been found far from any seacoast. This indicates that our late paleolithic ancestors were familiar with long distance travel, that trade routes had been mapped out and marked, and that trade and safe passage agreements may have been negotiated among different groups of humans. These negotiations may have required such complex social skills as learning another group's language or dialect and becoming familiar with their customs.

Long-distance trade facilitated the widespread transmission and adoption of new technologies. So once the late paleolithic advance picked up momentum, stability and continuity replaced the fragile and sporadic nature of earlier developments. Information about a new dye pigment or cutting tool, for example, would spread throughout a large geographical region. This eventually eliminated the danger that an innovation would be lost, and allowed advances to build on one another.

The extensive catalog of late paleolithic advances shows clearly that something significant had happened to *homo sapiens*. We were beginning to come into our own as the dominant animal species on planet earth.

Tool innovations and the resulting population expansion had important consequences. Starting about 32,000 years ago the archaeological record shows an increase in the number of skeletons of woolly mammoths, the largest and most prized prey, killed by late paleolithic hunting equipment. As more were killed, the population and the range of woolly mammoths began to dwindle. The last small isolated herd of these magnificent animals lived on Wrangel Island, a remote Russian territory in the Arctic Ocean. Interestingly, the last remaining herd only became completely extinct about 4,000 years ago.

The populations of Neanderthals and Denisovans, two earlier species of the genus *homo* that inhabited Eurasia longer than our own species, also dwindled around this time and then became extinct. Their extinction may be related to the decreased availability of wooly mammoths, because this was also their favorite prey. It may be that their more primitive hunting techniques could not compete with *homo sapiens* and our superior late paleolithic hunting technology. These earlier species may also have been less able to adapt to changing circumstances – switching to new types of food, for example. The last Neanderthals probably lived in present-day Spain around 30,000 years ago. They are not entirely gone, however, because there was a small amount of interbreeding between Neanderthals and modern humans, and about 4% of our DNA is Neanderthal. Some interbreeding apparently occurred with Denisovans as well, but what became of them is not yet clear. Meanwhile, as we continued to flourish and live longer, *homo sapiens* spread out to new areas, eventually migrating south to Australia and east to Alaska and the Western Hemisphere.

Explaining the Advance

The paleolithic period ended 15,000 - 12,000 years ago, followed by the mesolithic period (middle stone age). And the development of agriculture, as grain began to be cultivated and farming communities began to be established, marked a transition to the neolithic period (new stone age) about 10,000 years ago. Agriculture and the domestication of farm animals made it possible for humans to live in much larger groups, leading to the creation of cities and towns. From then on, the pace of human social and technological development accelerated dramatically. Neolithic advances include the development of writing, the making of bread, cheese, wine and beer, and the sail. The wheel was not invented until about 5,500 years ago, because while they look simple, wheels and axels were actually a fairly complicated invention. By that time, humans in Eurasia were smelting copper and other metals, leaving the stone age behind. But all of these later developments were built on the foundation of innovation and creativity that began with the late paleolithic advance.

Most anthropologists feel that the upsurge of inventiveness that characterized the late paleolithic advance must have been propelled by some driving force. The strength and speed of this development requires an explanation.

The earliest explanation was that humans came to the full use of language around that time, and language accelerated our progress. But the evidence now shows fairly conclusively that language developed far earlier. That theory is no longer tenable.

Another early explanation was that while humans had language, the language they started out with was primarily gestural, similar to sign language, with vocal sounds only accompanying and augmenting the gestures. Since our hands were busy signing, they weren't available for making new things until the transition to primarily vocal language occurred. But the fact that early humans made and used hand-axes, cooked with fire, and undertook many other manual activities makes it highly improbable that their hands were too busy gesturing. Moreover, deaf people today who communicate primarily by signing do lots of other things with their hands as well. So this theory too has insurmountable weaknesses. Three other possible explanations are supported by more credible evidence.

Genetic Transfer

Anthropology professor David Anthony has proposed that genetic changes in humans, including some gene transfer as *homo sapiens* interbred to some extent with Neanderthals in Europe and Denisovans in Asia, precipitated the late paleolithic advance. According to this theory, because these other species had been living successfully in Eurasia far longer, incorporation of some of their well-adapted genetic material gave just the right boost to modern humans.

DNA analysis has confirmed that *homo sapiens* picked up some genetic alterations from interbreeding with Neanderthals and Denisovans around the right time period. These were probably useful for our survival in Eurasia in some ways, perhaps by providing resistance to local diseases, toleration of colder weather, and the ability to adjust to differences in the length of the day throughout the year. But is there a close connection between these genetic improvements and the scope of technological innovations we subsequently produced?

Even in our middle paleolithic period, *homo sapiens* technology was superior to Neanderthal technology. So what useful mental abilities could we have picked up from earlier species? The prime candidates are genes regulating the ability to hunt in close quarters by quickly anticipating how an animal will react. A gene called FoxP2 shows up in humans 42,000 years ago, which could have been picked up from Neanderthals and could have affected *homo sapiens* in this way. But by this time, *homo sapiens* had less need to hunt in close quarters. Our species was moving in the opposite direction, developing new ways to take down prey at greater and greater distances. So genetic transfer should be considered a partial explanation at best.

Environmental Push

Beginning about 45,000 years ago, the climate of Eurasia became much colder, culminating in what is referred to as the Last Glacial Maximum about 30,000 years ago. The amount and type of plants and animals for hunting and gathering changed drastically during this period. It is possible that this environmental change, and the corresponding need to hunt new prey and incorporate new foods into our diet, pushed paleolithic humans into using previously dormant cognitive abilities.

This type of environmental push may well explain, in a general way, why humans were searching for new technologies, and it may provide a driving force for the activation of previously dormant abilities. But some late paleolithic advances, like musical instruments, do not seem related to environmental adaptation. And more importantly, Pat Shipman pointed out a curious fact that the environmental push theory cannot explain. Not just one but two populations of meat-eaters were especially successful and experienced a significant increase during this same time period: humans and wolves.

Contact with Wolves

Wolves were the top carnivore in Eurasia prior to the arrival of humans, and during the middle paleolithic period wolves competed with humans for prey. The hunting paths of both species frequently overlapped, and humans and wolves probably fought over one another's kills.

These two predators probably intruded on one another in other ways as well. Wolves were sometimes killed by humans, especially for their fur, and humans, particularly children, were sometimes preyed on by wolves. Children were warned about this danger with tales about the "big bad wolf", such as the fairy tales collected by the Grimm brothers in the early 19th century.

The word "wolf" comes from an Old German word meaning "murderer" or "evil spirit."

7. The Big Bad Wolf Disguised as Grandma

But at some point one of the most fortuitous events in the history of life on earth occurred. Some human contacts with wolves became friendly, and this, eventually, led to some of them becoming dogs.

One possible connection between human contact with wolves and the late paleolithic advance is that the two species began co-hunting, and their combined abilities became an unbeatable combination in terms of bringing in large quantities of meat. On this theory, the resulting increase in the supply of nutrition to human brains, and perhaps the need to spend less time hunting, lifted us to a new level of invention and creativity.

But it is doubtful that true co-hunting occurred at or soon after the initial friendly contact between humans and wolves, or that friendly wolves were welcomed by humans because of an interest on the part of humans to co-hunt with wolves. The complexity of commands required for co-hunting would have taken a long time to develop. Although humans hunt in groups and wolves hunt in packs, there are significant differences in how they hunt. Wolves usually run their prey to exhaustion, and they run much faster than humans. Moreover, wolves raised within a human group would not know how to hunt unless they had been taught, because hunting is a learned behavior that adult wolves teach their young. Dog expert Mark Derr pointed out that "Wolves born and raised in captivity without exposure to wild wolves are fundamentally clueless about hunting and killing, because they have not been taught how" (p. 173).

Learning to communicate across species is a lengthy process. Today, hunting dogs are carefully selected and trained to respond to commands from a young age. Early humans could not have known how to select or train wolves or foreseen how such an investment would pay off in the future. There had to be a more immediate benefit.

It is more likely that wolves living with a human group came to serve a useful sentry or guard function. This theory, that increased security was the primary asset our ancestors found in the canines who became dogs, was initially proposed by Australian anthropologist Colin Groves and veterinarian and animal rights activist David Paxton, and was later expanded upon by animal psychologist Stanley Coren. In the introduction to his book *Pawprints of History*, Coren imagined the following scenario in which a paleolithic human is talking to his dog-wolf:

"My grandfathers heard you bark. Every time an animal or a man approached, you barked. What a wonderful thing, they thought. If you stayed close and barked, then nothing could surprise us in the dark. So to keep your family close, we threw extra food to you (p. xii)."

Our ancestors would have noticed that dog-wolves barked or growled when wild animals or strangers approached the outskirts of their settlements, and that this provided an alarm system. The dog-wolves were not aiming to benefit humans, but simply protecting their territory, as wolves had done for hundreds of thousands of years. They naturally made ideal sentries, and their descendants are still used that way today.

Dog-wolves may also have helped control vermin within the settlement and cleaned up the garbage. They may also have helped keep our ancestors warm on cold nights. But dog-wolves were especially useful at night for dealing with the threat of nocturnal predators. Canines have acute nighttime senses of hearing and smell and light sleeping habits. And they mark the perimeter of their territory, concentrating on points of intersection with the scent of animal paths, to warn other animals to keep their distance.

Once our ancestors began co-habiting with dog-wolves, the added security meant that they were able to sleep more deeply on a consistent basis. And secure sleep, in turn, allowed paleolithic humans to make fuller use of their cognitive ability. Thus, sleep security provides the best explanation for the late paleolithic advance and the most satisfactory solution to Wallace's Conundrum.

Environmental push and genetic transfer may also have played a supporting role. It may also be that increased human security was important, not only because of facilitating sleep, but because it lowered the rate of human death and injury. Some late paleolithic advances may have resulted from the simple fact that there were more people. But sleep security is the only theory that offers a specific mechanism to account for increases in human creativity and invention.

Sleep security may have also increased not only because of dogs, but as a result of the development of more substantial dwellings. This one advance, perhaps occurring at the same slow pace as previous developments, would have then precipitated the other advances. It is important to consider, though, that these dwellings, while a big improvement in weather protection, were still largely made from branches or bones and hides and were not all that secure against large and determined predators.

How did the sleep security provided by dogs facilitate creativity and inventiveness, ushering in the late paleolithic advance? To answer this question, we need to examine the critical role that sleep plays in regulating human cognitive functioning.

4

Sweet and Sour Dreams

What happens as we sleep is somewhat of a mystery to most of us. In our fast-paced world some people even consider sleep a luxury or a nuisance. Nevertheless we all sleep, and after sleeping we feel rested. Research on what happens during sleep can help us understand the importance of sleep security for *homo sapiens*.

We experience sleep as a quiet, inactive time, and on one level, that is what it is. Our metabolism slows down and behind-the-scenes restorative functions like muscle growth, tissue repair, and hormone release take place. For example, while we sleep our pituitary gland secretes prolactin, a hormone that promotes the growth of new nerve cells. Another restorative activity is that during sleep adenosine triphosphate (ATP) is cleared from our system. While we are awake our brain produces this chemical to fuel cell activity, but as ATP accumulates over the day, it begins to slow down the rate of brain activity, making us feel progressively more tired and drowsy. Caffeine blocks the action of ATP, which is how it keeps us alert, but the effect is temporary. Clearing ATP from our system prepares us for the next day.

But something besides rest is also going on while we sleep. Activity of critical importance is taking place in our brains. This is clear from the fact that infants and young children spend about 13 to 14 hours per day sleeping during the critical period when their brains are developing and integrating. Sleep makes possible the healthy cognitive functioning of our large brains.

Sleep and Cognitive Functioning

The human brain contains more neurons than there are stars in our galaxy – more than a hundred billion – and each neuron has thousands of connections, called synapses, with other neurons. These synapses are extraordinarily active, using up about 80% of the calories we take in every day. Much of this activity takes place in the prefrontal cortex, the part of our brain that exercises control over cognition and aspects of language and social behavior.

Our prefrontal cortex needs to take periodic breaks from all of this activity. Sleep allows this to happen. Monitoring of electrical activity has shown that two alternating sleep states reset our brains each night: slow wave (SW) sleep followed by rapid eye movement (REM) sleep. These sleep states alternate in cycles that last approximately 90 to 110 minutes and are repeated four to six times per night.

SW sleep is the more restorative sleep state, and REM sleep – defined by its characteristic eye movements, darting back and forth or up and down, stopping and starting again, often accompanied by small jerky movements of our limbs – is the more active state. REM sleep helps us integrate and make sense of each day's experiences by connecting them to information stored in memory. The more new experiences we have during the day, the longer we spend in REM sleep that night.

Dreaming occurs mostly during REM sleep. The amount of time we spend dreaming correlates with the time elapsed in REM sleep, and the eye movements and limb jerks in REM sleep roughly reflect what we dream about. For example, if we dream about running we might move our leg, while if we dream of punching someone, we might move our arm.

Connecting each day's experiences to stored information during sleep helps us organize our memory and consolidate new learning. It also helps us cope with daily emotional ups and downs and boosts our creativity and insight.

Memory

Each day we are exposed to much more information than we could ever store in our memory. And even if we could store this much information, it would take too much time for us to sort through it all and access the information needed for any particular situation.

So during sleep, we discard unimportant bits of information to make room for more the next day, and we categorize important ones so they can be retrieved later with a minimum of delay and confusion. Information is sorted by topic and filed away. This is sometimes called gist processing, because we are extracting the gist of an experience and connecting it to related memories. Dreaming helps by replaying and thus strengthening the most important memories.

Interestingly, gist processing has a negative as well as a positive side. As memories are consolidated, they can be modified and distorted. In one psychology study, sleep improved subjects' memory of peoples' faces, but it also caused them to incorrectly "remember" similar faces they had not previously seen. That is because rather than remembering every detail, the study subjects assigned faces to general categories based on similarities that they had previously determined were important. But even though false "memories" like this are unhelpful in some contexts – for example, they render some eyewitness testimony in criminal trials unreliable – the net effect is positive, because freedom from being mired in every detail of every experience lets us focus on what is most important.

Learning

Sleep gives us time to strengthen and store what we learn. In one sleep study, psychologists taught subjects a five-button key-press sequence on a keypad. They later tested the subjects and measured their speed and accuracy in performing the task. But one group learned the task in the evening, slept, and was tested in the morning; the other group learned the task in the morning and was tested in the evening, with no sleep in between. The group who had slept performed the task 20% faster and 35% more accurately than the other group.

Timing is important, though. If one does not sleep within 24 hours after learning something new, improvement in learning due to sleep is lost.

Emotional Regulation

We are more likely to remember emotionally arousing experiences than emotionally neutral ones. For example, we may see cars drive by our home all day and not remember any of them, but if a car accident occurs in front of our home, we will remember it in vivid detail. That is because as we sleep and dream we tend to categorize events by the importance of their emotional impact.

Cycles of REM sleep help us make sense of our negative experiences and thus diminish their emotional hold on us. The mind takes what is bothersome or perplexing and blends it with what is familiar. In this way, REM sleep can function as a mild form of self-therapy, helping us maintain emotional balance and making us more adaptively flexible during wakefulness.

Creativity and Insight

Sleep helps us identify patterns and make associations among memories, including novel associations we had not thought of while awake. In an ingenious experiment, subjects were given several statements that imply other statements. They were told, for example, that of four things, A is greater than B, B is greater than C, and C is greater than D. They were not specifically told that A must be greater than D, but it was implied by the other statements. One group learned the statements in the evening, slept, and was tested in the morning; the other group learned them in the morning and was tested in the evening. The group who slept was significantly more likely to correctly figure out the implied statement. Next, the subjects were taught to solve a complicated mathematics puzzle, then later were shown it again and asked to solve it. As before, half of them slept in between and half did not. What none of the subjects were told was that there was a hidden shortcut that would easily solve the puzzle. Almost everyone who slept figured out the shortcut, but none of those with no sleep did. The sleeping brains worked behind the scenes to look at the problem in a creative new way.

Dreaming

Dreaming is an integral part of the processing we do during sleep. During a typical lifetime, a person will spend an average of six years dreaming. Whereas awake perception travels into the brain from the external world through our senses, dreams originate within the dreamer's brain, and perceptual content is added from memory as the dreamer creates a story and fills it with scenes, actors and action.

As we progress through sleep cycles, our dreams may initially replay events during the day that are stored in short-term memory, but as the brain begins to add in associations and connections from long-term memories dreams become longer, more complex and less realistic. Objects and events can become symbolic, such as a life transition indicated by a bridge. Revisions from one dream to the next seem to function like multiple tellings of a story, helping us to see something from various perspectives.

Dreams also test out approaches to a problem by playing out alternative scenarios and bringing more information to bear on the places we get stuck. This allows us to refine strategies for dealing with problematic situations. For this reason, the majority of dreams are somewhat unpleasant. We have more sour dreams than sweet dreams. The things we need to figure out how to deal with are the things we worry about, and we construct dream scenarios from these worries.

Since the dreaming self has the freedom to make up events and characters that are impossible in the real world, contradictory beliefs and inconsistent scene switches are common in dreams. Such creative free-play helps us develop new insights and gives our thinking more flexibility. Often, if something is difficult to figure out, we sleep on it, and we may have the solution to the problem the next morning, after it has been considered by what John Steinbeck called the "committee of sleep" (p. 71).

A conversation between the dreaming self and the awake self is sometimes needed to figure out the solution to a problem. The following account is a good example. A high school student trying to decide whether to join the school softball team or concentrate on his studies and just watch the games with friends had the following dream: *I'm camping in an open area in a tent that doesn't go all the way to the ground. People are coming by and staring in at me. I feel uncomfortable and exposed.* Reflecting on the meaning of the dream the following day, the student concluded that it was telling him that he would not be happy just watching the games as a spectator. He should join the team.

Dream Incubation

Our awake and sleeping selves influence one another in other ways as well. Paying attention to one's dreams when awake can affect what we dream about. A contemporary Native American shaman explained that "If a person doesn't believe in his dreams... if one doesn't do what a dream has directed...one won't be able to dream well any more" (quoted in Snyder, p. 105). And we are more likely to recall something from a dream that we have consciously directed ourselves to remember.

It is also possible for the awake self to suggest dream topics to the sleeping self. People sometimes engage in ritual actions as they prepare for sleep intended to invite dreams on a particular topic. The effectiveness of such preparation, called dream incubation, has received some experimental confirmation.

In the ancient world, particular sacred or sanctuary places were set aside for dream incubation. The most famous was the Temple of Asclepius, the Greek God of Medicine, in Epidaurus, on the east coast of Greece. This Asklepeion was one of the major health care centers of the ancient world. A spring at that location was considered to have healing properties since prehistoric times, and a temple complex was constructed around it, with baths and shrines, where pilgrims would come to drink from the spring, offer gifts to Asclepius, then sleep and hope for the healing god to send them a dream message to help cure their illnesses.

Resident dogs were part of the sanctuary experience at the Asklepeion. They were available to sleep next to visitors during dream incubation. And as a practical treatment, the sanctuary dogs were employed to lick the wounds of those with flesh wounds. It was believed the saliva of a dog had curative powers. Modern research has validated the presence of antiseptic agents in canine saliva. The statue of Asclepius that once adorned the temple included a sanctuary dog lying at Asclepius' right foot.

8. The Temple of Asclepius, from "The History of Medicine" series by Robert Thom. From the collection of Michigan Medicine, University of Michigan, Gift of Pfizer, Inc., UMHS.5

The maladies that drew people to the Asklepeion most likely included things like anxiety, autism spectrum disorder, depression, and others that were poorly understood in those days. If so, dogs in the Asklepeion may have performed healing functions in ways not unlike today's therapy dogs. But we can only speculate.

The Meaning of Dreams

People in the ancient world practiced dream incubation, accompanied by religious rituals, because they believed that many dreams contained messages from the gods, a belief probably carried over from prehistory. They also believed that some dreams foretold future occurrences. We know this because Aristotle devoted two of his books to arguing against this view, as part of his project to construct a rationalistic and logical philosophical system. Aristotle believed that the content of dreams had almost no meaning.

Since we now know much more about the function of sleep, we can appreciate how a dream might provide us with new insights, such as when we go to sleep unable to solve a difficult problem but wake up with the perfect solution. This type of experience may be the source of the ancient belief that dreams were messages sent by the gods. And we know that dreamers sometimes rehearse alterative scenarios to deal with conflicts and problems. If we rehearse enough alternative scenarios, it is likely that one of them will actually happen. When it does, we may recall that we dreamed it, and take this as evidence that the dream foretold the future.

An ancient writer, Artimedorus, held a view not far removed from our modern conception of dreams. He wrote that most dreams are prompted by recent personally significant events during the day that then appear as dream images, stories and symbols. They can best be understood as messages from ourself to ourself. Artimedorus' book on dream interpretation, written around the year 140, contained chapters explaining the meaning of the various images, stories and symbols encountered in dreams. For example, he wrote that a serpent signifies one of three things: a king, because of its strength, a long life, because it is long and sheds its skin to become new, or wealth, because in many legends serpents guard treasure.

Sigmund Freud theorized that many dreams are expressions of unconscious childhood urges and conflicts. Contemporary research supports his central thesis that the dreams of people with serious inner conflicts very often arise from and play out these conflicts. Freud's pupil Carl Jung held a view of dreams more applicable to healthy everyday functioning. He believed that dreams are our attempts at achieving psychic wholeness.

Jung felt that there are two kinds of dreams. Ordinary dreams are specific to each individual's daily experience and personal history. The other kind, archetypal dreams, contain symbols and images common to all humanity, derived from our common biological heritage and universal human experiences, such as gaining adult independence or battling obstacles to reach a goal. These symbols and images form what Jung referred to as the collective unconscious, which he believed was the source of myths and icons recognizable in some form across all human cultures.

Jung's understanding of the meaning of dreams was influenced by several visits to traditional, pre-literate societies; first the Taos and Pueblo communities in New Mexico and later Kenya and Uganda. He learned that these societies paid careful attention to dreams and had complex views of the relationship between dream time and awake time. Such traditional perspectives may provide a window into how our paleolithic ancestors might have viewed sleep and dreams.

Dream interpretation today is a thriving business. Numerous books and websites claim to unlock the secrets of dreams. Their popularity speaks to the high level of interest and wide diversity of viewpoints on their meaning in our modern world.

Sleep Duration and Quality

To receive the benefits of sleeping and dreaming, we need to sleep long enough and soundly enough. The average adult human needs between 7.5 and 8.5 hours of sleep per night, but some people can function with 7 or fewer hours' sleep, while others are better off with 9 hours or more.

Quality is just as important as quantity. Sleep requires a sense of safety to remain intact. Interruptions block the progression of sleep cycles, and sleep that is too light has the same effect. While nobody completely disconnects from the external world during sleep – smoke detector alarms are set at a volume loud enough to waken almost anyone from a deep sleep – the control gate that allows sense perceptions to enter the brain can close to varying degrees, leading to a higher or a lower arousal threshold for the sleeper. A sleeper with a low arousal threshold experiences a light sleep, remaining somewhat alert to many kinds of external stimuli. But sleep that is too light is as detrimental as interrupted sleep.

Sleep Deprivation

When we are unable to achieve a state of deep sleep for a sufficient amount of time, the resulting deprivation has serious negative effects. It slows our reaction time and lowers our frustration tolerance. We react more impulsively and become more mentally rigid. Even a one-hour reduction in sleep over several days causes a sleep debt serious enough to damage our performance and thinking.

Sleep-deprived people may fall asleep in dangerous circumstances. Some people even fall into what is called a micro-sleep, lasting from a fraction of a second to up to 30 seconds. The head nods and eyelids droop, often without the person being aware of it. And lack of sleep can precipitate mood swings and even emotional disturbance, as emotions swing from extreme annoyance to extreme giddiness in a matter of moments. These effects are not just harmful to the individual. They cost society a great deal in lost productivity, medical expenses, and accidents.

Disorders such as insomnia, restless leg syndrome and sleep apnea have a negative effect on our sleep, but sleep deprivation precipitated by the environment rather than internal causes has the same negative effect. For example, people working in some occupations are at risk of being deprived of adequate sleep. Military personnel on combat missions must often endure days with no or only sporadic sleep. The Department of Defense has created a Sleep Research Center to better understand the effects of sleep deprivation on combat readiness. The Center's studies have revealed serious problems, including impulsive decisions, slow reaction times, impaired communication and comprehension, incomplete task performance, and forgetting important details.

Sleep deprivation can have devastating consequences. During the Battle of Savo Island in World War II, Japanese naval and air forces attacked a U.S. battleship fleet near the Solomon Islands in the Pacific Ocean just after midnight on August 9, 1942. The sailors manning the fleet, fatigued from several nights of constant alertness, reacted slowly and made multiple mistakes. Four ships were lost, four others were damaged, and 1,077 U.S. sailors were killed, as compared with 58 Japanese losses. Many consider this the worst naval defeat in U.S. history. A naval inquiry blamed the defeat primarily on insufficient sleep.

Some civilian occupations expose workers to dangerous levels of sleep deprivation as well. Truck drivers and airline pilots, for example, are at risk of becoming overtired during their work shift, and sleep deprivation is a major cause of accidents. Hospital personnel sometimes also work such long hours that their sleep is insufficient for exercising good judgment and performance. One survey of almost 20,000 doctors in their first year of hospital residency found that those who had worked for 24 hours straight or more were twice as likely to be involved in an automobile accident on the way home as those working a shorter shift.

Secure sleep is also difficult to maintain in some living environments, particularly disadvantaged urban neighbor-hoods. Living conditions such as crowding, residential noise, gang violence and other criminal activity reduce the amount and quality of sleep residents are able to obtain. Children are especially affected. Researchers analyzing data from the 2007 National Survey of Children's Health found that only 36% of children living in socially disadvantaged neighborhoods received adequate sleep each night during a typical week.

Studies have documented the negative impact of such chaotic living conditions on children. Research specialists at the U.S. Department of Health and Human Services have found that children in high poverty areas with inadequate sleep were four times more likely to experience behavior problems, including not getting along with other children and being disrespectful of teachers and neighbors.

Family psychologists Eleanor Brown and Christine Low examined the impact of poor sleep on the academic functioning of children in disadvantaged neighborhoods. A group of children with adequate sleep and a group with poor sleep were both given a puzzle and a tower task to complete. For the puzzle task, researchers gave children one easy and one difficult puzzle, then measured their persistence on the task and asked which puzzle the children would like to do again. Children with poor sleep kept at the task for a shorter length of time and more often preferred the easier puzzle the second time. For the tower task, they gave children blocks and asked them to estimate how high they could build a tower with them, then had them build a tower. Those with poor sleep underestimated their skill at tower building. This points to a tendency towards diminished motivation and achievement for the sleep deprived group that can persist throughout an individual's life.

Another group of people who experience sleep difficulties is nighttime caregivers for infants, children with health problems or disabilities, or aging relatives. About two thirds of children with physical disabilities need assistance during the night, for example, and the parents of 49% of children with developmental disabilities report being woken up four nights a week or more for caregiving duties. Although the sleep loss on any given night may be brief, nighttime caregivers typically maintain a low arousal threshold, remaining only half-asleep and vigilant enough to wake to the first whimpers of their babies, for example.

Frequent sleep interruptions and maintenance of a low arousal threshold has a negative impact over time on mood, stress levels, and overall health, and leads to serious cognitive performance deficits including slower information processing speed and greater difficulty learning new tasks. Even a brief sleep interruption three times per week has as serious a detrimental effect as only getting five hours or less of sleep per night. Working mothers with interrupted sleep have reported difficulties functioning at their jobs.

Sleep Security

There are instructive parallels between the sleep insecurity we have been considering and two other security problems people sometimes face: housing and food insecurity. People with housing insecurity are not homeless but are chronically anxious about having a place to live and face issues like moving often, living with relatives or friends or in overcrowded dwellings, or dealing with eviction or utility shutoff notices. Similarly, food insecurity is not hunger or malnutrition, but a chronic concern about having enough to eat, running out of food, or having no alternative to an unhealthy diet. The negative effects associated with each of these problems include stress, feelings of helplessness, and health problems. Children in families who experience housing insecurity, for example, are almost twice as likely to experience developmental delays.

In the same way, sleep insecurity, characterized by periodic interruption, maintaining a half-asleep form of vigilance at night, and/or being worried about nighttime safety, is detrimental to daytime functioning. Such problems may be so routine that they are not even recognized. And the impairment resulting from sleep insecurity may be so subtle that it is not consciously identified as being related to sleep. But these experiences take their toll nonetheless. Adequate secure sleep is essential for us to face life's challenges with creativity and flexibility.

Humans go to enormous lengths to ensure the safety and security of their sleep. To deal with internally-generated sleep disturbances, an estimated one in four American adults takes sleep medications. To deal with externally-induced causes, regulations limit the length of work shifts of truck drivers, airline pilots and hospital personnel. The military has issued regulations to help minimize sleep problems for combatants as much as possible. And respite care programs provided by disability service organizations give nighttime caregivers needed breaks, allowing them to temporarily relax their vigilance and catch up on needed sleep. Through my work as a rehabilitation counselor I became aware of the critical importance of providing this type of support to the families of children with disabilities.

In their daily lives, many people have bedtime routines designed to encourage relaxation and help prepare for sleep, such as taking a bath, fluffing up a favorite pillow, reading in bed or watching a familiar TV show. We prepare children for sleep by changing into pajamas, telling stories, singing lullabies, and so on. Night-lights and special stuffed animals or blankets help children feel safe at night.

And today many people have elaborate home security systems to ensure their nighttime security. But the world's most widely used security system, today and throughout history, is the family dog. Excavations of Pompeii – the ancient Roman city destroyed in the year 79 by the eruption of Mount Vesuvius – revealed several mosaics at home entrances with pictures showing a fierce dog, sometimes along with the words *Cave Canem*: Beware of the Dog.

9. Beware of Dog Mosaic, Ruins of Pompeii

Dogs provide security because their sleep patterns are different from ours. They take naps throughout the day and sleep in a way that allows them to become instantly alert when they hear or smell something unfamiliar, and to settle back down when things around them are calm. Their arousal threshold is naturally lower than ours, and their dreams are shorter and simpler.

While there are numerous contemporary stories of dogs warning of and even attacking intruders, many of us today have family dogs whose security function could best be described as ceremonial, such as barking at the garbage truck. Yet we may still feel a special sense of peace and security when they lay near us, a feeling that is not connected logically to any contemporary behaviors or experiences, but is real nonetheless. And the fact that dogs tend to warn us of dangers that are not really there, like the garbage truck, also means that they are unlikely to fail to warn us of real dangers, and that in itself is comforting.

Our family dog Poco sleeps on our bed with his head at the foot of the bed, facing the most likely source of danger. The head of the bed is against the wall, with the foot facing the window. When

Poco barks at night, I let him know what it is, if I can – e.g. "It's just the wind" – or if I don't know, I ask him to investigate, and if he persists, I get up as well and check it out. Once I say "It's OK," we go back to sleep. We expect this type of partnership from one another.

10. Poco Defending the Front Door against All Enemies, Foreign, Domestic, and Imaginary

Interestingly, the two animals that humans today most frequently respond to with intense fear – spiders and snakes – are the two sometimes deadly animals that approach with no sound or scent, so dogs aren't good at protecting us from them. This suggests that our hard-wired fears have been shaped over the millennia at the biological level in tandem with our co-habitation with dogs. Our sense of being safe and guarded is a part of the profound connection humans and dogs have formed with one another over tens of thousands of years.

Sleep During Paleolithic Times

Since there is no difference between the brains of paleolithic and modern humans, adequate sleep was as critical for their optimal functioning as it is for ours. But paleolithic sleep was much more vulnerable to externally-induced sleep disruption.

As *homo sapiens* spread throughout Eurasia, they hunted animals for meat but were also themselves sometimes hunted by formidable predators. These included several species of large cat that used stealth tactics to hunt at night: cave lions 50% larger than today's African lions, a tiger-sized saber-toothed cat called a scimtar cat, and leopards similar to those in Africa today.

Nighttime must have been frightening back then. After dark our most acute sense, eyesight, was limited to the immediate area surrounding a campfire. Our diminished sense of smell made it difficult for us to detect nocturnal predators. Author David Randall summarized the situation as follows: "With no sharp claws or teeth to scare off potential predators, early humans were at their most defenseless when they laid down on the ground for several hours in the middle of the night" (p. 244).

All of the ancient predators except wolves and black bears were gone from Europe by about 25,000 years ago. Today, with fewer and smaller remaining predators and far more substantial dwellings, most of us are better protected. However, it was not long ago that some humans still had reason to fear large nocturnal cats. British records from the time they ruled India – 1858 to 1947 – listed an average of 1,500 human deaths from tigers and other large predator cats per year.

The sleep insecurity faced by nighttime caregivers may be the closest contemporary analogy to the situation faced by paleolithic humans who needed to remain alert to periodic nocturnal dangers. In the same way that parents must maintain a low enough sleep arousal threshold to ensure that they can be aware of a child's nighttime epileptic seizure, for example, in paleolithic times adults needed to be vigilant enough to thwart attacks from predators. They no doubt often wound up with poor quality sleep.

During paleolithic times, our *homo sapiens* supercomputing brains had the potential to make all sorts of discoveries and inventions, but that could only happen if we were able to obtain sufficient secure sleep for the background processing such brains require. Until this problem was solved, early humans were held back. Compared to people today, these ancestors of ours were more mentally rigid and less creative. Sleep insecurity led to Wallace's Conundrum, a puzzling gap between the time we emerged as a species and the time we began making serious developmental advances.

Paleolithic people would not have experienced this, of course, because the way they functioned was normal for them and an advance over anything that had come before. They had no higher standard to judge their performance against. Even people today whose sleep is mildly insufficient or interrupted often do not report feeling sleepy or subjectively experience that their performance, memory and judgment are sub-optimal. But if their sleep improves, they are amazed at the difference.

An important key to the remarkable late paleolithic achievements of our ancestors was the sleep security provided by the ancestors of dogs. And although it is unlikely that paleolithic people made the connection at the time, it is clear that they did recognize and esteem the role that their canine companions played as the sentries and guardians of their safety.

5

Guardians of the Spirit World

It is easy to imagine paleolithic humans doing exactly what we do today: Puzzling over a problem in the evening, then falling asleep and perhaps having a fresh perspective on the matter the next morning. But many of their problems were different from ours. Perhaps they were trying to figure out how to make arrows fly straight or clay pots more durable. During deep sleep, safely guarded by a dog sentry, the brain might make a new association, such as between an arrow flying and a bird flying, or might recall a stored memory of a clay pot that became harder on the side closer to the fire. These associations could provide the insights needed to add tail feathers to an arrow or to pit-fire a clay pot. Sleep security gave our ancestors the full benefits of sleeping and dreaming.

But what did our ancestors think was happening to them when they fell asleep and dreamed? Many of us today are interested in figuring out what our dreams mean and how they might apply to our waking life, but our paleolithic ancestors may have viewed dreams far differently than we do. Direct knowledge is impossible to obtain, but we can piece together a rough idea of what early humans may have experienced from some indirect sources.

The Spirit World

Ancient historical accounts of sleep and dreams are available to us that probably derived from far earlier traditions, and thus may provide some insight into the worldview of paleolithic people. We also have access to information about how sleep and dreams are understood in contemporary societies that have not been influenced much by modern cultures. Carl Jung, dissatisfied with the scientific accounts of dreaming available in his day, visited Native American elders and tribal villagers Africa to deepen his understanding. Such traditional cultures are more likely to carry forward ancient traditions and beliefs. We can base some reasonable speculations on these two indirect sources of information.

It is likely that paleolithic people believed that much of what we think of as happening inside of our minds was located in a spirit world. The spirit world was also outside of conventional space and time, but nevertheless was as real as any other part of the world. The Prashna Upanishad, an ancient Hindu scripture, expounded the view that sleep is closer in some ways to ultimate reality than is wakefulness.

According to this view, dreams, for our paleolithic ancestors, were a form of soul travel to the spirit world. When falling asleep, we may sometimes have the sensation of being taken away from ourselves. So it is not difficult to imagine early humans viewing dreaming as a trip to another realm of reality. This would have given dreams a legitimacy and seriousness for them that we can scarcely imagine. Nighttime travel to the spirit world served three important functions.

Guidance for the Group

A dream could provide guidance not just for the dreamer but for their whole social group. The aboriginal people of Australia are said to make a distinction between little and big dreams. Little dreams relate to narrow personal concerns, but in big dreams, the dreamer is dreaming for the whole community. For example, a dream might indicate where animal herds are headed, or who is best suited to become the next leader of the group. The distinction between these two kinds of dreams is similar to Jung's distinction between ordinary dreams and archetypal dreams.

Because of their potential importance for the community, dream interpretation was not left to the individual dreamer but was the province of specialized mediators often called shamans. The term "shaman" originated with Siberian peoples but is now used as an umbrella term for similar roles found across many cultures, such as "medicine man," "seer," "wizard," and "oracle." Dreams were reported to the shaman, who might then meet with the elders of the group to discuss their meaning. Keeping a dream to oneself was unheard of, and would have been a serious violation of one's social responsibility.

Healing and Resolving Difficulties

Dreams were thought to provide insight into all sorts of physical maladies and clues to their resolution. Sick people used dream incubation to try to focus their dreams on their specific situation, and this eventually led to the development of healing centers like the Asklepeion in ancient Greece. In tribal societies, healing based on the dream was a central role of the shaman, whose interpretation of the spiritual forces acting upon an individual was used to select rituals, medicinal plants and other treatments. Even such everyday problems as what sort of love magic to use to attract a romantic partner were within the scope of the shaman role.

Shamans also treated psychological difficulties. We have seen that a degree of anxiety and confusion inevitably accompanies having a large brain, and the psychological costs imposed on us by our extraordinary cognitive powers and intensively group-connected lifestyles have always needed to be addressed. Today, we tend to view the need for spiritual healing and psychological guidance as the purview of counseling or psychotherapy. But psychological health as understood by early humans probably had little to do with self-realization or personal growth, as we think of those things today. The work of the shaman was in the context of helping people realize and fulfill their proper role within the group.

Visiting with Spirits

Since the first awareness of death arose in us at the dawn of our emergence as a species, we have noticed a relationship between sleep and death. "Sleep" is commonly used as a euphemism for death, as when we speak of putting an animal to sleep. Shakespeare called sleep "the death of each day's life." And in ancient Greek mythology Hypnos, the god of sleep, and Thanatos, the god of death, were twin brothers.

Deceased people sometimes appear in dreams, and the dreamer seems to carry on a relationship with them. This was understood during paleolithic times as the dreaming self visiting with the spirits of the ancestors. By com-municating with ancestral spirits, one could receive guidance and comfort from those who had completed the full arc of human life.

Animals were thought to have spirits as well. Early humans were keen observers of other animals and the distinctive qualities or powers that each animal possessed: courage, craftiness, loyalty, and so on. In dreams, humans believed that they could meet these spirits and learn to participate more fully in those qualities. There could also have been a special relationship, as there was in Native American cultures, between a particular human and a particular "totemic animal." By adopting the animal's name, such as "Sitting Bull" or "Black Elk," the human could share in some of their power.

Paleolithic humans most likely believed that they could also gain access to the spirit world through other means besides dreaming. Much artwork, such as depicting animals in cave paintings, and activities like dancing and playing music may have been used to call upon and placate spirits. Dreamlike states could be achieved through trances, visions, and altered forms of consciousness brought on through rhythmic dancing or repetitive chanting, singing, and drumming. Some deep caves may have been selected for their almost unearthly-sounding acoustic properties or for their ability to induce a state of sensory deprivation, transporting people into the spirit world. There is evidence of wear on hollow stalactites and stalagmites in some caves dating from paleolithic times, indicating that they may have been used as percussion instruments. Altered consciousness may also have been induced though hallucinogenic plants. Some geometric patterns on cave walls and stone artifacts – spirals, undulating lines, and checkerboard patterns – are remarkably similar to drawings produced by contemporary people recalling hallucinatory experiences.

Guardian Spirits

Beginning in paleolithic times, stories and images reported through dreams and trances became incorporated into the cultures of human groups and became the legends and myths that helped people make sense of their world. In traditional societies, such legends and myths and associated rituals and dances were passed down and perhaps embellished from one generation to the next. Animals played important roles in the legends and myths of many cultures, and people often dressed up like particular animals to enact rituals and recite stories.

One of the animals that played a particularly important role in myths about the spirit world across many different cultures is our familiar companion, the dog. In the *Epic of Gilgamesh* from ancient Mesopotamia (about 4,000 years ago), dogs are the companions of the goddess Innana (Ishtar).

The role that has been most consistently associated with the dog is that of sentry or guardian. Legends and myths across the world and throughout history speak of the importance of dog spirits as the guardians of humans.

In some Tibetan Buddhist monasteries, a dog is brought into the room of a dying monk to guard the soul until it can be reincarnated in a new human body. And in many cultures, dog spirits are assigned the role of safeguarding our permanent sleep just as they guard our nighttime sleep. In fact, according to one ancient African myth, dogs are responsible for the fact that we humans remain permanently dead. At one point, dogs were sent by the gods to fetch humans back from the dead, but the dogs became distracted by the enticing pile of bones they found, and forgot what their mission was.

According to the Vendidad, a 2,500-year old collection of Zoroastrian myths, prayers and religious observances, a dog's gaze is considered to have the power to ward off demons. Zoroastrians also believed that the bridge to heaven was guarded by dogs, and they required a dog to be present at a funeral so that its spirit could guide the deceased individual's spirit across. Dog-lovers will be happy to know that these guardian dogs made sure that nobody who had abused a dog could enter heaven unless the individual had made atonement.

The ancient Greeks and Romans believed that Cerberus, a three-headed hound, guarded the entrance to Hades to make sure the spirits of the dead don't return back to earth. In early Hinduism, dogs provided a similar function. The *Rig Veda*, Sanskrit hymns composed in India an estimated 4,000 years ago, contains the following verse: "Draw nigh then to the gracious minded fathers... and those two dogs of thine...the watchers, who guard the path and look after men. Entrust this man to their protection" (Book 10, Hymn XIV).

In Norse mythology, the watchdog Gamyr guarded the gate to the underworld. Dogs performed a similar guard function in Welsh mythology.

In Mexico, the Aztecs developed a special breed of dogs called Xolos, associated with the doglike deity Xolotl, guardian of the underworld. People would often be buried with their Xolos by their sides, freshly sacrificed, to help guide them to the underworld.

The ancient Egyptians also imagined a canine creature as the guardian of the underworld. Anubis – sometimes depicted as a dog, sometimes as a jackal, or a man with a jackal's head – guided human spirits to their final resting place.

11. Face Time: Osiris and Anubis

The fact that myths about dog spirits as guardians are deeply embedded in human cultures points to the sentry function as being one of the most salient qualities we associate with dogs. This is powerful evidence that something about the way dogs were seen as guarding us, and especially our sleep, has stood out as exceptionally important for humans since prehistoric times.

But the ancestors of dogs that paleolithic humans first welcomed into their settlements were not yet today's dogs. To reach that point, and to cultivate the relationship we now have with one another, both species had to embark on a long and fascinating journey.

6

Domestication

Biologists have known for about a century that dogs are descended from the grey wolf: *canis lupus*. However, it is only since the development of DNA analysis in the mid 1980s that they came to understand that dogs *are* wolves. The internationally accepted reference source on mammal species, *Mammal Species of the World*, reclassified the dog in 1993 from *canis familiaris* (domestic dog) to *canis lupus* (wolf). Dogs are now considered a sub-species or variety of wolf: *canis lupus familiaris*.

An even more recent development has been the recognition of how long ago our association with dogs began. We have known that dogs were our companions before cats, and before we domesticated goats, horses, sheep, chickens or cattle. Anthropologists originally assumed that human population growth, spurred by the development of agriculture at the dawn of the neolithic era, brought wolves sniffing around early towns and cities. But new evidence has shown that we were co-habiting with dogs long before we developed agriculture.

One type of evidence supporting an earlier date is the fact that an earlier date is now recognized for when the human groups that spread from Asia to the Americas separated from those that remained in Asia. DNA studies now place that separation at 25,000 to 20,000 years ago. Since *canis lupus familiaris* accompanied humans to the Americas – and met the Mayflower passengers on their first day ashore – dogs and humans must have been companions prior to that separation.

But it has come as a surprise how much earlier. Evidence has been uncovered from five separate archaeological sites of domestic dogs living with humans around the time of the late paleolithic advance.

Site 1 is Predmosti, near today's city of Prerov in the Czech Republic, occupied by paleolithic humans 27,000 – 26,000 years ago. Three skulls found at Predmosti were identified in 1977 as dogs. Their shorter skulls and snouts and wider palates and braincases resemble contemporary dogs more closely than contemporary wolves. Archaeologists dismissed this finding when it was first presented, believing that it must have been an error. Refusing to see what does not fit with one's preconceptions is more common in science than you might suppose. We saw that Boris Levinson encountered the same refusal to acknowledge the evidence he presented about the therapeutic effectiveness of dogs. Recent re-analysis of the Predmosti skulls using more refined techniques in the 1990s confirmed that they are those of dogs.

Site 2 is the Chauvet Cave in southern France. In addition to spectacular cave paintings on the walls, two sets of footprints from about 26,000 years ago were discovered preserved in the soft clay floor. One set of footprints was made by a barefoot boy perhaps 8 – 10 years old, and the set of prints alongside the boy's are from an early dog-wolf. The prints show that the boy was walking normally, not running, and that the dog-wolf was walking alongside, not tracking or stalking the boy. The boy was probably carrying a torch and stopped at some point to scrape off some charcoal, which provided the material for carbon dating.

Kimberly Patton, historian of ancient religious practices at the Harvard Divinity School, has identified the Chauvet Cave as a prehistoric site for dream incubation. She believes that the acoustic properties of the cave and paintings on the walls may have been connected with rituals involving calling upon the spirits of ancestors and animals.

Site 3 is the Razboinichya Cave in the Altai Mountains, where China, Russia, Mongolia and Kazakhstan come together. The skull of a canine living with humans around 33,000 years ago was unearthed there and DNA samples were compared with the DNA of wolves living in the same region around the same time and with the DNA of contemporary dogs. The Altai Mountain skull was more closely related to dogs than to wolves. A separation between the wolves who had begun breeding with one another to eventually become dogs and those who remained wild had to occur more than 33,000 years ago in order to show up as clear DNA differences.

Site 4 is in the Taimyr Peninsula in central Siberia. The genome from a 35,000-year old canid was sequenced, and this individual too, like the one at the Razboinichya Cave, had already begun diverging from the common ancestor of dogs and present-day wolves. This specimen was most likely an early ancestor of the modern Siberian husky and Greenland sled dog. Interestingly, central Siberia is also where shamanism is thought to have originated, and around this same time period.

Site 5 is the Goyet Cave in Belgium. DNA analysis of a skull originally dated at about 32,000 years ago shows that it was clearly different from the skulls of wolves and closely resembled the DNA of much later dogs. A re-analysis of the same samples with more sophisticated techniques has now dated this skull even earlier, to about 36,000 years ago.

The archaeological evidence from these five sites provides us with an "at least as long ago" date for humans living with dogs, since future finds may push dates farther back. However, there is always the possibility of error when artifacts are analyzed. There was likely a long period during which wild wolves and tame wolves interbred to some extent, and there are also other species of the genus *canis* such as coyotes, jackals, and extinct animals called dholes that are easily confused with and can occasionally interbreed with wolves. This creates difficulties in proving to which species a particular bone or skull belongs. In addition, canid bones could be found with human bones for several different reasons. It does not necessarily mean that the two animals were companions. The relationship might have been one of predation, or the two could have lived and died years apart and never interacted.

Because determining the date of our first co-habitation with the ancestors of dogs is partly a matter of interpretation, not everyone agrees with a paleolithic time frame. Darcy Morey, professor of anthropology at Virginia's Radford University, expressed a concern about the accuracy of some of the dating methods. Cornell University's Abby Grace Drake and her colleagues also disputed the earlier dates. Based on re-analysis of the Goyet Cave skulls using conventional skull measurement techniques, they believe that the skulls more closely resemble wolves than dogs. It should be remembered, however, that evolutionary change is very slow. The ancestors of dogs would have had to co-habit with humans for a very long time before their skull shapes changed to a measurable degree. DNA changes would show up sooner, and DNA analysis is widely accepted as a reliable dating method.

Archaeology is a dynamic field, with new finds being continually unearthed and dating methods continually improved. It is not surprising that there are competing opinions on when the ancestors of dogs first came into our lives. But the findings across the five sites identified so far are remarkably consistent. Evolutionary biologist Olaf Thalmann estimated an earliest date of 32,100 years ago and latest date of 18,800 years ago for the origin of the domestic dog. Evolutionary geneticist Dr. Love

Dalen at the Swedish Museum of Natural History, in an interview with BBC News, offered the opinion "that the split between dogs and wolves happened around 30,000 years ago seems fairly definitive." And based on her review of the scientific literature to date, Penn State Anthropologist Pat Shipman concluded that "... by about 36,000 years ago, there was a distinctive group of large canids that showed up unusually often in sites made by humans" (p. 222). The preponderance of evidence currently available points to consistent human/dog co-habitation in Eurasia around the time the late paleolithic advance got underway.

Initial Contact

When humans first met them, wolves had been the top Eurasian predator for a long time. They were superb hunters due to their effective pack hunting tactics. One tactic was to run their prey to exhaustion by staging small groups of wolves at strategic intervals along a path of pursuit. Each group steered the prey towards the next group, which would then take over the chase. Wolves also mastered the tactics of decoy attacks, where one small group would drive the prey towards the rest of the pack, and the tactic of driving prey over a cliff or into water.

As humans joined wolves as a second top predator in Eurasia, during the middle paleolithic period, the two species crossed paths often, because they were after the same prey. They also preyed on one another to some extent.

But at some point, something improbable and unprecedented happened. A few of these fierce competitors began to be friendly towards one another. Perhaps a couple of wolves came sniffing around human kill sites or settlements at mealtime, to sneak off with some scraps of meat or see if they could get at a discarded carcass. They mostly kept their distance or were chased away. But one or two wolves who were especially friendly – perhaps wolf pups who had not yet developed a sufficient wariness of danger – persisted in hanging around, came a little closer than usual, and their presence was tolerated. The flight distance of a wolf – the distance maintained from an animal that is unfamiliar and a potential threat – is unusually low to begin with. In addition, wolf pups are curious and playful. The friendliest ones came closest and were most likely to get some food scraps, and they probably kept coming back.

Perhaps the initial contact was with human children, who are also curious and playful and less cognizant of danger. Extended childhoods gave children ample time to play and explore. Perhaps a child began playing with a wolf pup and then became the first in a long line of children to look pleadingly into the eyes of his or her parents and ask, "Can we keep him?"

After the initial contact, however it happened, a group of humans must have come to tolerate the fairly regular presence of a friendly wolf or two. It would not have taken long before they noticed that these newcomers performed valuable services. They helped with waste management by cleaning up leftover food scraps and bones. And their acute senses of smell and hearing made them especially alert in ways that humans are not, and this turned out to be an early warning capability protecting against the big cats and other paleolithic dangers.

Eventually, a tentative connection was formed between some tolerant, curious humans and some friendly, curious wolves. A wolf or two, no doubt appreciating regular access to cooked meat, adopted a group of humans as its social group, stuck around, and stayed all night. Once several friendly wolves began to spend much of their time around a human group, they tended to breed more with one another than with the local wild wolf population. As this trend continued, interbreeding occurred with greater regularity with each succeeding generation, and this eventually led to the friendly wolves becoming a distinct genetic population.

Once humans and dog-wolves were used to one another, they began at some point to experiment with hunting collaboratively. The results were spectacularly successful. As Shipman noted, "Hunters working with dogs clearly find more prey, find prey faster, and bring home more meat" (p. 186). William Dansey, in the 1831 Appendix to his translation of the ancient Roman work *Cynegeticus* (hunting with dogs), waxed poetic about the benefits of the dog/human hunting alliance:

> Short of due perfection were all the hunter's wiles, till the dog was tutored to assist in the sylvan pursuit and massacre, and to contribute the acuteness of his senses, his speed and courage to the service of mankind, who consummated their superiority over the animals of the forest when they had directed to the chase the adapted powers of this faithful ally (p. 183).

From that point on, our ancestors and the descendants of a sub-population of wolves lived together, worked together, improved their communication with one another and became inseparable partners. They were so successful, in fact, that the populations of prey they hunted started to decline in numbers, some species being completely wiped out, and this was followed closely by a decline in the populations of other predators, who saw their food supply dwindle.

Becoming Dogs

The process by which friendly wolves became tamer and developed into dogs as we know them today is known as domestication. But this is an imprecise way of characterizing the process. First, it suggests deliberate human activity. With other domestic animals, that is the case, but dog domestication was probably accidental on our part, and probably initiated by wolves.

And second, as wolves turned into dogs, they changed humans to a degree that no other animal ever has. Domestication, if that is what we want to call it, proceeded in both directions.

Once a somewhat distinct population of dog-wolves became regular members of a human group, humans would have favored the friendliest and most useful ones in each generation by making sure they had the best scraps of meat. Those who were too aggressive would have been refused food and chased away, to become reabsorbed into the local wolf population, or killed. Those favored would have remained with the group and mated with one another. Eventually all dog-wolves were relatively friendly and nonaggressive towards their human companions.

Our ancestors most likely had no idea that the traits they favored in dog-wolves were more likely to be passed on to their offspring and that this would create a distinct sub-species after many generations. Someone may have deliberately matched two especially well-liked dog-wolves for breeding purposes, but there would not have been an overall plan or goal. Deliberate breeding is fairly recent. Nonetheless, without anyone knowing what they were doing, the behavior of dog-wolves was shaped over time so that it came to exhibit more and more the behavior that meshed best with human behavior. Dog-wolves became wolf-dogs. They went from being tolerated to being welcome and then to being indispensable.

After many hundreds of generations, dog-wolf DNA and the DNA of wild wolves had diverged enough so that the difference was detectable through DNA analysis. Over many more hundreds of generations, physical changes that accompanied the behavioral and genetic changes became noticeable, including the skull differences we see today, and a sub-species of canis lupus became clearly recognizable as dogs: *canis lupus familiaris*. But although these changes made a critical difference, only about 0.04% of the dog genome has evolved. The dog is still 99.96% wolf.

It is important to keep in mind how gradual the process of domestication was, with no clear dividing line between wolves and dogs. The process can be viewed as occurring along a continuum, with arbitrary names given to some of the stages. For example:

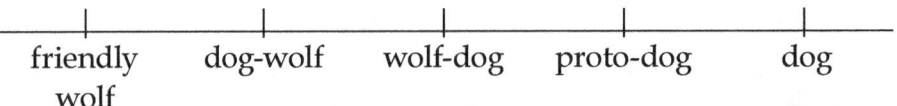

friendly   dog-wolf   wolf-dog   proto-dog   dog
wolf

Over time, humans became more and more accustomed to relying on dog-wolves and then wolf-dogs to participate in a wide array of activities, and they, for their part, became more and more attuned to responding to the movements and emotions of their human companions, as well as increasingly dependent on them for their survival. Today, what are sometimes called feral dogs – those who have reverted to a wild state – indirectly depend on humans by scavenging most of their food near human settlements. There is no stable dog population anywhere living completely independently of humans, and thus it is more accurate to say there are no truly feral dogs. "Feral dog" is an oxymoron.

In terms of physical characteristics, compared with the average wolf the average dog is somewhat smaller overall, with a more rounded head, a cranium about 15 percent smaller, larger eyes, and smaller teeth. Dogs also have a shortened face and a more pronounced angle between the forehead and the nose. Shortened faces allow many dog breeds to see with binocular vision, like humans do, rather than looking to each side with a blind spot in the middle, like wolves do.

Most dogs also have an accentuated sclera, or white outer covering of the eyeball, which perhaps evolved to augment their ability to communicate. White eyeballs allow the direction of gaze of the pupil to be visible to observers. Humans and dogs are the only animals whose eyes have clearly visible white eyeballs. Humans can tell where other humans are looking and where dogs are looking, and dogs can tell where humans are looking and where other dogs looking. This gives our two species the ability to read one anothers' gaze signals and makes us uniquely effective communication partners for co-hunting and other activities.

As part of their friendly disposition, dogs look at humans and at one another as a greeting and communication signal – something no other animal does. This naturally gives us humans the feeling of being personally greeted and attended to by a dog.

Behaviorally, dogs are far more docile than wolves, since we favored the friendliest ones. Dogs also reach sexual maturity earlier and display more sexual behavior, mounting and mating outside of the traditional wolf reproductive season. One theory is that heightened sexual behavior served as a type of replacement behavior for reduced aggression.

Dogs also continue as adults to behave in some ways characteristic of juvenile wolves, with playfulness, curiosity, and a lot of tail-wagging and barking. Wolf cubs bark often but adult wolves only bark occasionally, to alert the rest of the pack to a serious danger. Tail-wagging and barking in a variety of circumstances, as we see in today's dogs, may be side-effects of favoring the friendliest animals. The frequency of barking may also have increased as wolves became dogs simply because they joined us in being very vocal.

Evolutionary changes involving some adult characteristics and behaviors coming to resemble those of juvenile ancestors is called neoteny, a process we have come across earlier in connection with another species: *homo sapiens*. Some people have assumed that looking and acting like juveniles was consciously selected for during domestication, so dogs would look cuter and make more cuddly pets. But it is more likely that what was selected for was friendliness alone, and all of the other changes, while appreciated, were side-effects.

Evidence that this is the case came from an unlikely source. Beginning in the early 1950s the Russian zoologist Dmitri Belayev led a research team in a breeding experiment with another canid species – silver foxes – in what was then the Soviet Union. Belayev was based in the city of Novosibirsk in Siberia, which coincidentally is the same region where we have seen that one of the earliest dogs was discovered and where shamanism originated. His research design involved letting one group of foxes breed normally, but for another randomly selected experimental group, only allowing the foxes friendliest to humans to mate with one another each season. The study proceeded in this way for over two decades. For much of this time Belayev and his team had to mask their experiment to fool government authorities about what they were doing, since Soviet Union policies forbade studies like this and Belayev risked imprisonment if his true purpose was discovered. In the Stalinist era, all genetics research had to conform to the crackpot ideas of a Soviet scientist named Trofim Lysenko, who opposed this type of experiment.

After about 20 generations, the foxes in Belayev's experimental group were consistently friendly and tame towards humans, whereas the other group continued to be just as fearful of humans as silver foxes are in the wild. This finding was expected, but an additional surprising finding was that the foxes in the experimental group were also different in other ways. They reached sexual maturity earlier, so that adults retained some juvenile features and behavior, they maintained longer breeding season than the other group, and they had shorter and wider faces. This seems to demonstrate that such features appear on their own in canid species as side effects of selecting for friendliness.

Belayev's team began to document changes in foxes after about 20 generations, but that was under experimentally controlled conditions using scientific breeding techniques. It is difficult to know how long it took for a sub-population of wolves to become dogs using the informal, unplanned selection process that would have taken place during paleolithic times. Penn State anthropologist Pat Shipman regards 40 - 45 generations as the minimum amount of time that would have been needed to accomplish behavioral domestication, with a longer time needed to produce genetic and observable physical changes.

The real-world domestication process was probably very drawn out. Dog co-habitation with humans may have begun more than once, with friendly wolves hanging around human settlements but breeding regularly with other wild wolves as well as with one another, and perhaps fading back into a wild state one or multiple times before co-habitation became exclusive. Domestication from wolf to dog-wolf, wolf-dog, proto-dog, and finally dog with measurable skull differences may have taken a thousand generations or more.

As the ancestors of dogs became established within one or more groups of humans, word of their usefulness got around. Perhaps puppies would be given as gifts when human groups met one another. Once wolf-dogs and then proto-dogs became a stable feature of human lifestyles, any human groups without them would have found themselves at a disadvantage in protecting themselves and competing for food. Eventually, and continuing up to today, all human groups included dogs.

Human Domestication

Domestication worked both ways. As a sub-population of wolves became dogs, humans changed as well. In the late 1990s, Australian veterinary scientist Jonica Newby and anthropologist Colin Groves proposed the theory that dogs and humans domesticated one another. Dr. Newby wrote and presented a series of programs on animal domestication on Australian television and later joined the Australian Broadcast Company as Science Editor. This groundbreaking theory has subsequently been supported by further evidence.

One step towards domestication was that paleolithic humans picked up useful hunting tactics by observing and then co-hunting with the ancestors of dogs. Co-hunting gave us access to more protein in our diet and enough food to support a larger population.

Our observation of wolf pack behavior may also have taught us something else. Paleolithic humans, with almost no built-in instincts but unparalleled built-in cognitive ability, paid a great deal of attention to observing the behavior of other animals. This allowed our ancestors to better find those that were prey and avoid those that preyed on them. Jeffrey Masson, a New Zealand animal rights activist and expert on the emotional lives of animals, has theorized that as we humans observed some of the instinctive social behavior of dog-wolves, we picked up valuable information about successful social living. Wolf behavior is exceptionally social and cooperative. For example, wolves share available food among everyone in the pack, take turns minding young pups, and protect the pack at any cost, even to the extent of sacrificing their own lives if necessary. They also settle disputes easily among themselves. A wolf will snarl or gently nip another wolf when annoyed, whereupon the offending wolf will quickly apologize for any unintended infraction, and the annoyed animal will respond equally quickly with behavior indicating forgiveness. In this way, the inevitable disputes occasioned by living in packs never get out of hand.

This trait of instant forgiveness may help shed some light on why it is that dogs are often characterized as being nonjudgmental. We have seen that this somewhat simplistic belief is commonly put forward as an explanation for the effectiveness of therapy and service dogs. Dogs, while not truly nonjudgmental, do share with other wolves the behavior of instant forgiveness, a response that begins and ends so quickly that it might appear to humans as practically the same thing as being nonjudgmental.

Humans may have incorporated social behaviors identified through observation of our dog-wolf and wolf-dog companions into our codes of morality. Jeffrey Masson noted that, "the closest approximation to human morality found in nature is the gray wolf" (p. 52). It could be said that we have been trying with mixed success to master these social behaviors ever since. Mark Derr also considers it likely that our partnership with canines is responsible for some of our sophisticated social behavior. Referring to such behavior, he noted that, "That is not primate behavior. That is wolf behavior" (p. 125).

Just as those wolf-dogs and proto-dogs more adapted to living and communicating with us had more reproductive success, humans who were more skilled at interacting with canine companions – for example, those more patient in training them or more flexible in adapting to their instinctive behaviors when co-hunting – were better off than those who were not. Over time, as the ancestors of dogs became tamer, so did our ancestors.

By far the most significant changes to humans as a result of our domestication by dogs resulted from their service as nighttime guards and sentries. Secure sleep allowed us to take advantage of our cognitive functioning ability as never before, unleashing the inventive and creative potential of the human brain. In this way, dog/human co-habitation ushered in an era of unprecedented progress. Complex tool-making, access to more and more varied food, better shelter and clothing, the beginnings of art and science, and all of the other late paleolithic advances that took place during such a short period of time that they have amazed anthropologists had their roots in this era. And, as a side effect, through experiencing dogs as a source of safety, humans began to develop a biological response of increased calm and peacefulness in their presence.

As co-domestication proceeded, other biological changes took place as well. Dogs and humans came to share many of the same diseases, including obesity, obsessive-compulsive disorder, epilepsy, and some cancers. The genes that control digestion in dogs have adapted to digest the foods humans enjoy better than the diet of wolves. This is part of the reason why what are called feral dogs today primarily eat scavenged human food. They can no longer hunt like wild wolves or digest the diet of wild wolves.

Comparisons of the dog and human genomes over time show that in our two species, our sequences for reduced aggressive behavior, neurotransmitters like serotonin, and digestive processes like cholesterol processing have been evolving in parallel for many thousands of years. Such parallel genetic changes in two different species are extremely rare, and are evidence of a long history of close companionship.

Through co-domestication, humans and dogs both look into one anothers' eyes when interacting. And oxytocin levels increase both in both partners, as the oxytocin increase in each partner causes an increase in the other partner's oxytocin level. We have seen that oxytocin, a hormone transmitted through the central nervous system to the bloodstream, produces feelings of well-being. Cats and some other pets can also cause oxytocin release in humans, but there is no evidence of an interspecies oxytocin feedback loop with any two species other than dogs and humans. This feedback loop helps produce the powerful documented effects of therapy and service dogs, and is the same feedback loop that occurs with human babies and their mothers to help create a strong emotional bond between them. Both feedback loops have survival value.

No pictures of the scene were taken, but I am willing to bet that when Charlie lept up into President Kennedy's lap during the Cuban Missile Crisis, he looked up into President Kennedy's eyes, and President Kennedy looked down into Charlie's eyes. And in that moment, perhaps, the world was saved from nuclear destruction.

The dog/human interspecies hormone feedback loop is a clear reminder of how long the bond between our two species has been developing and how strong the biological connection between dogs and humans has become. As Australian veterinarian David Paxton put it, "part of what defines a human being is an association with dogs, and vice versa" (p. 7). By domesticating one another, we extended one anothers' abilities over time in ways that allowed our two species to collaborate in an extraordinarily wide range of activities.

7

Here's Looking at You

From the earliest days of the dog/human partnership, each species took advantage of ways in which the other's abilities complement and extend its own. Of primary importance for humans was the fact that a dog's senses of hearing and smell provide information about the environment that our own senses cannot match. We also benefit from the fact that dogs have a remarkable social awareness that allows both species to interact easily.

Dog Senses

Humans have better eyesight than dogs, but dogs hear and smell things that we cannot. Interestingly, dog sentries are often called "watchdogs," but whereas human sentries would have no choice but to rely primarily on their sense of sight, dogs don't do a lot of watching. They listen and sniff.

Sense of Hearing

The hearing of dogs and humans begins at about the same low frequency, about 20 hertz (the standard sound wave unit), but dog hearing spans a range up to 45,000 hertz or more, depending on the dog's age and breed, whereas humans can only hear sounds up to about 23,000 hertz. A dog whistle, for example, produces a high-pitched sound out of range for humans but only slightly above the middle of the range for dogs.

Another source of better hearing in dogs is their earflaps. With 18 muscles for each ear, most dogs can position their ears to better collect and localize a sound. There are differences across breeds, however. Some dogs have been bred to have floppy ears, which limit their range of motion.

The average dog can hear sounds coming from about four times farther away than the average human. And in addition to greater range, distance, and directionality, a dog's brain also detects other subtle sonic qualities that we can't notice.

Sense of Smell

Dogs have 125 - 300 million scent glands within their nasal cavities, depending on the breed. By contrast, a human has about 5 million scent glands. And dogs can move each nostril independently, giving them directional information about smells. Dogs can also collect air in a special chamber of their nose that stays there when the dog exhales, so scent molecules can accumulate until there is a sufficient concentration for the dog to identify an odor.

The part of a dog's brain that processes smell is 40 times larger than in human brains. An estimated one-third of the dog's brain is devoted to scenting. Besides being able to discriminate different smells, a dog has an excellent olfactory memory.

As a result, a dog's sense of smell has been estimated to be 1,000 to 100,000 times more sensitive than a human's, depending on the breed and the specific chemicals being scented. In one study dogs even detected the presence of a test chemical called eugenol at one-millionth the concentration that humans could. So when your dog greets you, he or she probably knows where you have been, who you have been with, and what you have been eating and drinking.

And your dog probably also knows what mood you are in, perhaps with better awareness than you yourself. Inside the nasal cavity and opening into the upper part of the mouth is a small organ called Jacobson's Organ. This organ primarily detects chemicals called pheromones that provide dogs with information they need for breeding, but it also allows them to sense other chemicals. For example, they can smell adrenaline, the fight-or-flight hormone activated when we are fearful or anxious. It is likely that dogs can even smell sadness. This ability might help explain why Sigmund Freud's dog Jofi responded differently to patients with different types of psychological problems. Dogs can smell high blood sugar levels and can be taught to alert people with diabetes when the concentration becomes too high. Dogs have even been known to smell cancer on people, alerting them to it and saving their lives.

Social Awareness

In addition to superior hearing and smell, dogs have social skills that even our genetically closest relatives, chimpanzees and bonobos, do not have, and that we ourselves may have learned from them to some degree. These instinctive skills were developed long ago as wolves evolved to live and hunt in packs, and developed even further as the most friendly animals were favored by humans over tens of millennia, so that now the social behavior of dogs surpasses that of wild wolves.

Dogs read our facial expressions, gestures and body language, allowing them to understand our intentions and anticipate our actions to a remarkable degree. Psychologists Monique Udell at Oregon State University and Clive Wynne at the University of Florida provided the following summary: "Dogs...are exquisite readers of our behavior. Dogs do not need to be preprogrammed with responses to human gestures or actions, because they are incredibly flexible and quick to make associations in their environment" (p. 322).

Dogs are so good at these things that psychologists trying to design experiments to study them complain about it. Ivan Pavlov, who formulated the principles of classical conditioning in the 1920s by training dogs to salivate at the sound of a bell, explained how frustrating the process was for him because his dogs kept ruining the experiments:

> The experimenter, however still he might try to be, was a constant source of a large number of stimuli. His slightest movements – a blink of the eyelids or movement of the eyes, posture, respiration, and so on – all acted as stimuli which, when falling upon the dog, were sufficient to vitiate the experiments (p. 20).

Whenever dogs interact with or observe a human, even for a very short time, they learn to pick up on the smallest details of the human's behavior. They know where we are looking, and respond to and imitate our movements. The next time you and a dog are looking at one another, try this experiment: Blink your eyes a couple of times and the dog will blink back.

Making Eye Contact

We have seen that dogs and humans have co-evolved so that our direction of gaze is visible to them, as theirs is to us. Dogs are masters at using this ability to monitor what we see to interact with us.

Experiments have shown that a dog will drop a ball to a person's front, not the back, and a dog will ask for food from a person whose head and eyes are visible, but not from one whose head is hidden from them. A dog will stay away from an available food item it has been told it is not allowed to have if his or her master can see the dog, or if the dog knows that the human can see the food. When neither is the case, the dog chows down.

Wild wolves, by contrast, interpret being looked at as hostility. And they do not watch humans as a way of signifying friendliness. It makes them more aggressive. As a result, only rarely can a wolf communicate with humans effectively.

A research team at Eotvos Lorand University in Budapest, Hungary led by Adam Miklosi conducted an experiment to demonstrate this difference. They gave some tasks to nine dogs and seven wolves, designing the tasks so that the animals would be able to figure out how to complete half of them but not the other half. To prepare for the experiment they made sure that the background experiences of the dogs and wolves were as similar as possible by having the wolves live with human families from the time they were puppies and raising them like dogs are usually raised; i.e. close contact with humans, regular walks on a leash, and basic obedience training.

The first two tasks involved opening a bin to get a piece of meat and pulling a rope out of a cage to get a piece of meat attached to the end. All of the dogs and wolves figured out how to complete both tasks in 10 minutes or less. But for the next two tasks, the bin couldn't be opened, and the rope was tied to the back of the cage and couldn't be pulled out. When faced with tasks they wanted to complete but could not, seven of the nine dogs looked back at the human who was conducting the experiment, but only two of the seven wolves did. And of those who looked back, the dogs looked sooner and spent more time looking than the wolves. Miklosi's team concluded that a key difference between wolves and dogs is the dogs' readiness to look at the human face for guidance. This difference seems to be genetic and not something that can be altered by raising a wolf in a social environment.

Dogs initiate eye contact as a communicative signal. And if more than one human is present – one who is attentive to them and one who appears inattentive or preoccupied with something else – they initiate eye contact with the more attentive one. Wolves initiate eye contact for significantly longer periods of time than foxes and other canid species, but dogs gaze twice as long on average as wolves.

Responding to Movements and Gestures

Dogs respond readily to changes in human body posture, facial expression, voice tone, and other movements. For example, they follow human gestures like pointing. A dog will find hidden food or a hidden desired object if a human points to it, even when the human is walking away from it.

Much of our speech is accompanied by characteristic movements, voice tones, and/or bodily postures. We may not be conscious of these accompaniments, attending primarily to the content of what we are saying. But dogs do just the opposite, using available nonverbal information to make guesses about the content as it applies to them.

Likewise, many of our actions follow a predictable, habitual sequence. If I get up from working on the computer, for example, our family dog Poco can tell somehow whether I am leaving for only a minute or two and will be returning, or I am finished working for the time being. If I will be coming back, he doesn't get up, but if I am finished, he accompanies me, hoping for a walk outside. Like Ivan Pavlov, I found that it is no use trying to fool him. Dogs read behavior patterns and movements so slight we are not aware of them.

Learning Through Imitation

While dogs are not particularly good at solving problems on their own, they can learn to solve problems by watching people or other dogs solve them and then imitating their actions. In an experiment conducted by Monique Udell and her colleagues, humans showed two dogs a treat, then took one of the dogs, but not the other, around a section of fence to show them how to obtain the treat. When they placed both dogs back at the starting point, the dog shown the way went back that way to get the treat and got it more quickly than the dog shown the treat but not the way around the fence.

In another experiment, Udell trained dogs to perform several tricks, such as spinning in a circle. She then gave a single demonstration of a completely new trick, such as carrying an object from one place to another. In response to the simple command "Do it," the dogs correctly imitated the new action with 70% accuracy.

Some dog cognition experts believe that the acute sensitivity of dogs to human social cues may have been selected for during domestication. In other words, humans more often allowed dogs to breed who were better at responding to our social cues. But Udell believes that a simpler explanation is also plausible. She and her colleagues have argued that the only trait that needed to be selected for in dogs was increased friendliness. We have already seen that as a result of selecting for just this one trait, dogs, as a side effect, remain puppies longer.

According to this explanation, a longer period of puppy-hood keeps dogs in closer proximity to and more dependent on humans during the critical first few weeks when they are most impressionable, and this allows them to be more thoroughly influenced and socialized by their human companions. As a result, by the time they reach maturity, dogs have become virtuosos at reading human social cues and fitting in as members of human social groups, without the need for deliberate selection for that behavior.

There is some evidence for each explanation. Cognitive scientists Brian Hare and Vanessa Woods found that even shelter dogs reared without much human contact or training were skilled at reading human gestures. This would tend to indicate that this skill had been inbred. But it might also mean that dogs are able to learn these responses very quickly, even with minimal contact or training. For now, neither explanation can be ruled out.

Language and Communication

Dogs have impressive receptive language skills. They can learn to respond correctly to hundreds of words, and have been known to retrieve over 200 different items on command. Even more remarkably, an experimental group of dogs asked to retrieve an unfamiliar item after hearing its name for only the first time were accurate about 70% of the time. Most likely, they remembered which items already had other names, from retrieving them previously, and chose each time from only the smaller set of items they had not already identified.

Dogs also understand that objects can be placed into categories and subcategories. Randomly selected dogs were given objects in three categories: frisbees, balls, and a miscellaneous set of other things. The dog was then asked to "bring me a frisbee" or "bring me a ball", and rewarded for bringing an object from the correct category. After a few learning trials, the dogs always selected an object from the correct category.

Moreover, dogs understand that pictorial symbols can be used to represent objects as well as spoken words. In an elaboration of the previous experiment, dogs shown a miniature replica or only a photograph of an object always retrieved the correct object. Because the ability to group things into categories and then represent the categories symbolically is at the core of conceptual thinking, these experiments suggest that at least to a rudimentary degree dogs can form and use concepts.

Dogs can also learn the names for things without being specifically taught, simply by hearing humans talk about them, a process called incidental learning. I know this from my own experience. Spook, one of my family's first dogs, got so excited when she heard the word "out" that whenever a member of the family was not going to take her out immediately, we tried not to say the word. We started spelling "o-u-t" instead, so as not to get her hopes up. But after only a few repetitions Spook figured out that "o-u-t" meant "out".

Scottish novelist Sir Walter Scott believed that his dogs understood a great deal of what he said to them, and he talked to them in much the same way as he would to a human. He felt that "If people would speak slowly and with emphasis to their dogs, they would understand a great deal" (quoted in Coren, p. 87). When another famous author, Washington Irving, paid Scott a visit, they went for a walk with Scott's dogs and discussed the literary world of the day. Irving wrote home that he was impressed by the way Scott would "Frequently pause in conversation to notice his dogs and speak to them as if they were rational companions, and indeed there appears to be a vast deal of rationality that these faithful attendants of man derived from their close intimacy with him" (quoted in Coren, p. 86).

There is obviously a limit to what a dog can understand, and Sir Walter Scott's view may have been overly optimistic. But a dog can certainly understand the meaning of a sentence like "Not now, I have to finish my coffee first" – not in the same way we understand the sentence, but as it relates to them. If you say the same sentence consistently in the same context, in about the same voice tone, accompanied by the same behavior (ignoring the dog's request to play), after a few repetitions the dog will stop asking to play until you finish your coffee.

In general, whenever sounds are regularly paired with something else in a dog's experience, the dog will connect the two things. But the sounds have to be nearly the same each time. For example, if you say "Go find it" then when the dog brings the object back say "Good dog, you found it," the dog can't connect "find" and "found" because they sound different. If instead you say, "Go find it" then when the dog brings the object back you say, "Did you find it? Good dog," the dog will learn more quickly what "find" means. Similarly, "Let's go up" and "Let's go down" are easier to teach than "Let's go upstairs" and "Let's go downstairs," because words with the same last syllable aren't different enough. Maintaining the same voice tone is even more important than the words themselves. And talking to dogs about things that the dog cannot possibly relate to their experience is probably counterproductive. It tends to result in a dog who tunes out verbal content and thus comes to understand less than he or she otherwise might.

Since the words themselves are irrelevant, there is no need to teach a dog using an unnatural command like "Stay", when a dog will just as easily respond to a more natural request like "Hold on a minute." If Poco is far away and I want him to come to me, I don't say "Come," I stretch out my arms and call out "Run like the wind, Poco!" and he is next to me in no time. Instead of being surprised that Sir Walter Scott talked to his dogs in natural sentences, I wonder why Washington Irving wasn't surprised that many other dog "owners" talk to their dogs unnaturally.

As far as expressive communication – producing language – is concerned, dogs communicate primarily by means of nonverbal signals and gestures like head and eye movements, body language, and tail wagging. For example, dogs lower their heads and front legs in a gesture known as a "play bow" to indicate that they would like to play a game. Many dogs alternate looking at a human then at an object or location to indicate "showing" behavior. Similarly, dogs request help by looking at us, then at their problem.

Dogs are physically limited in the range of vocalizations they can make, but they do use a surprisingly large variety of different barks, growls, and whines to communicate all sorts of things. To just take one example, Poco has at least the following different growls: an attention-getting growl that means something like "Hey I need attention too you know," a play growl that means "Look how fiercely I am pulling on this toy," a frustrated growl that means something like "You are taking way too long," and a menacing growl in response to noticing a strange noise or an unexpected object. Dogs have a similarly wide range of barks and whines. The more success they have with communicating with a human partner, the harder they try to communicate. Just as our dreams are more meaningful the more we pay attention to them, our dogs tell us more the more we respond to what they tell us.

As we humans learned to take advantage of the ways in which a dog's senses of hearing and smell extend the reach of our own senses, and of their acute social awareness and ability to communicate, we asked them to join us in an increasing variety of roles. Dogs still keep us safe and warm and clean up dropped food, as they have for 30,000 years, and whenever their human partner needs them to help herd or hunt, they are happy to lend a paw. But today, they do much more besides.

8

Varieties of Canid Experience

The way their abilities mesh with and complement ours has allowed dogs to perform a wide variety of companion roles with humans throughout the millennia. Breeding has also produced many sub-types of dogs suited for specialized roles.

Beginning with the first co-habitation with their wolf ancestors, dogs helped with waste management, kept us warm on cold nights and served as sentries to keep evildoers away. Legends and myths from long ago and around the world speak to the importance of this protective role, and dogs continue to serve today as the nighttime alarm system for most humans.

Doggie Duties

Another valuable collaboration since paleolithic times has been as co-hunters. Dogs use their speed and acute senses to help find, chase after and retrieve prey. Once dogs were an established part of human society, they became indispensible on a hunt. In Greek mythology, Zeus' daughter Artemis, the Goddess of the Hunt, is usually depicted accompanied by her hunting dog.

ARTEMIS.

12. Artemis, Goddess of the Hunt, and Companion

And long before antibiotics and disinfectants were discovered, dogs helped keep wounds from becoming infected by licking them. As the millennia progressed, we asked them to partner with us in many other ways as well.

Herding

After we transitioned to the neolithic period and began raising sheep, cattle and other animals, dogs found a new niche, helping to control and guard other domestic animals. Shepherds were bred for that purpose. Experiences with dog domestication may have helped humans learn about the process of breeding to increase desirable traits in these other animals.

Work Animals

Since ancient times, dogs have provided transportation for people by pulling dogsleds and portage for goods as pack animals. Dogs have also performed a variety of other types of work, such as serving as "turnspit dogs" walking in circles to press cider, raise water from a well, or turn a rotisserie to roast meat.

Military Service

Arrian, in his book on dogs written in about the year 110, explained how the Anatolian forces, in today's Turkey, used fighting dogs in warfare. "The horsemen...were each accompanied to the field with a fighting dog, the dogs first collectively assaulting the enemy, backed by the foot soldiers, and lastly by the cavalry" (p. 238). Genghis Khan reportedly included 30,000 Tibetan mastiffs in the fighting force he used to invade Europe. And armies around the world today make use of dogs for important assignments.

Entertainment and Sacrifice

Dogs have also historically been used for entertainment purposes, mostly banned as exploitative today but still practiced in some places. Dog racing has been popular in many different cultures. In the US, the popularity of greyhound racing has declined precipitously in recent years and only a few states still allow it.

Dogfighting dates back to at least the 5th century BC, and still is practiced in some places. And bulldogs were originally bred for participating in a sport called bull-baiting, which was popular for a time in England. Spectators would watch a bulldog and a bull enraged with pepper-spray fight one another.

Dogs have sometimes been raised for meat, and still are in some places, most notably in South Korea, where restaurants offer dog meat on their menus. Dogs have also been sometimes sacrificed for their fur and as an emergency food supply, as we saw in the case of the Maori people of New Zealand. And the Aztecs sacrificed dogs as a religious ritual.

In modern times, dogs added several new services to their resumes.

Search, Rescue and Cadaver Dogs

Dogs are employed to rescue people from building collapses and other mass casualty events and natural disasters, in cooperation with local, state or federal emergency personnel. Rescue dogs are trained to risk their lives to comb through unstable terrain and detect human scents. Avalanche dogs can detect people buried by avalanches, and St. Bernard dogs were bred in the Swiss Alps primarily for that purpose.

13. Searching for Earthquake Survivors

Dogs also play an important role in searching for missing people and human remains. Search dogs learn to follow a systematic pattern and use air-sniffing to detect and then hone in on a scent they are looking for, often obtained from a missing person's clothing, and track the scent where it leads. Cadaver dogs can find human remains buried as many as 15 feet underground and skeletal remains over a hundred years old.

Detection Dogs

Most police agencies have at least one K-9 dog, most often used for suspect apprehension and for detecting narcotics or explosives. Dogs trained and certified through the Canine Training Center operated by the federal Bureau of Alcohol, Tobacco, Firearms and Explosives are capable of detecting up to 19,000 explosive chemicals. They can also detect traces of the accelerant chemicals used in arson. Dogs can be misled, however, into pointing out false positives – indicating, for example, that drugs are there when they are not – because of the way they can be influenced by their handlers' suspicions.

And as society has become more complex and modern humans often feel the need for a renewed sense of community, dogs have been there for us as well.

Companionship

The things we fret about and judge one another for – a bodily imperfection, a social blunder, and so on – we can count on our dogs to ignore completely. They know that the important thing, the only really important thing, is for two friends to just enjoy being together. Dogs provide companionship and sometimes serve as substitute objects of nurturing as families have fewer children and spend more time in an empty nest. Dog "ownership" is increasing in those parts of the world where families are getting smaller.

Connections with Nature

The family dog provides many people with an excuse and motivation to get outdoors more, get more exercise, and prevent what author Richard Louv has called "nature deficit disorder." Connections with the natural world and opportunities to notice outdoor sights, sounds and smells are directly linked to our mental and physical health.

Dogs also connect us more fully to our own animal natures. Many share the opinion that British psychoanalyst Mikita Brottman expressed about her dog: "He makes his bed wherever he happens to lie down. He has no shame about toilet functions. His lack of self-consciousness makes him a joy to watch" (p. 228).

Social Catalysts

Dogs make excellent conversation starters, or social catalysts, helping humans make contact with strangers. A study conducted in London's parks found that spontaneous social interactions were initiated with 2% of people strolling along with no dog, but with 25% of those accompanied by a dog.

One dog even used her conversation-starting personality to serve as an anthropology research assistant. Anthropologist Kate Swanson was doing fieldwork in Quito, Ecuador, attempting to understand the situation of poor street children, and she found that it was difficult to get her subjects to trust her enough to talk to her. Kate's dog Kiva quickly stepped in and began playing with the children, and Swanson found that they were happy to talk with her while they played with Kiva.

Therapy and Service Dogs

We have seen that therapy dogs assist people recovering from post-traumatic stress syndrome or traumatic brain injuries, those who have difficulties remaining focused and in control of their behavior, those who need to feel safe and relaxed enough to talk about their troubles, and those who want to be more sociable and more active. And service dogs assist individuals with their mobility and community functioning or provide early detection for things like dangerous blood glucose levels in individuals with diabetes.

And now we can see what makes therapy and service dogs so effective. Having examined how acutely sensitive dogs are to our behavior - to the point of noticing movements we are hardly aware of ourselves, how responsive they are to our emotions and moods, how readily they forgive mistakes, how prominently their role as our guardians is woven into the fabric of human culture, and how wide a range of activities our two species collaborate in, we can fill in with greater clarity the explanation that we previously glimpsed in only a rudimentary way. The secure sleep provided by dogs that helped ignite the late paleolithic advance also incorporated an almost magical calming effect into our biology. The built-in sensitivity of dogs to our movements and gestures is as affirming for us as it is frustrating sometimes to psychologists who want to study them.

Boris Levinson speculated that the naturalness and lack of inhibition of his dog Jingles benefitted children with emotional disabilities by giving them the freedom to talk about what bothered them and get down on the floor and roll around, if they needed to, without being criticized. And because dogs respond to humans in straightforward and uncomplicated ways, Olga Solomon saw that their easily interpretable behavior allowed individuals on the autism spectrum to feel more competent and develop more fully. But although these positive effects are especially noticeable and especially important for individuals who have disabilities, they are not limited to any particular group. Solomon noted that the unique ways that dogs relate to humans benefits anyone, with or without a disability. What dogs offer, they offer to any of us. We all respond positively to the spontaneity and simplicity that dogs bring to our lives.

Dog Breeds

Individual dogs differ widely from one another in their various abilities, just as individual members of any species do. Selective breeding by humans has also resulted in dogs being more diverse than other mammals by a considerable margin. *Canis lupus familiaris* has the widest variation in size, appearance, and behavior of any variety of animal. When humans began intentionally breeding dogs, they emphasized characteristics most suited to the specialized purposes they had in mind, developing shepherds for herding sheep and retrievers for retrieving game, for example. The purposes of some dogs have been mostly forgotten nowadays, such as the keeshond chasing rats away from the cheeses loaded on canal boats in the Netherlands. But while we may no longer know their purpose, the dogs still know. Our retriever Maggie used to employ her specialized abilities to help us garden. Whenever we found stones in the garden, we threw them out into the surrounding weeds. Maggie considered it her solemn duty to locate each stone and place it back in the garden.

Over many generations of breeding, different varieties of dogs emerged. In ancient Roman times, Flavius Arrian recognized just three types: *pugnaces* - fighting ones, *sagaces* - smart ones, and *celeres* - fast ones. A somewhat larger number of breeds was recognized by Shakespeare's time, judging from these lines from *Macbeth*, Act 3, Scene 1:

Hounds and greyhounds, mongrels, spaniels, curs,

Shoughs, water-rugs and demi-wolves are cloped

All by the name of dogs; the valued file

Distinguishes the swift, the slow, the subtle,

The housekeeper, the hunter, every one

According to the gift which bounteous nature

Hath in him closed; whereby he does receive

Particular addition, from the bill

That writes them all alike.

By the 19th century, people began to formally keep records of canine ancestries and to classify dogs into more narrowly focused breeds rather than broad functional types. Most of the breeds we recognize today originated less than 150 years ago.

More than 400 dog breeds are now recognized by and registered with organizations like the American Kennel Club, which hold dog shows, field trials, and other events measuring quality and ability. The first dog show was held in 1887 in England. Interestingly, though, despite vast differences in appearance and behavior, few cognitive differences have been found across dog breeds.

Breeding today is a controversial business. Show breeders intentionally select for traits which they claim are improving a breed, yet many of the traits being emphasized seem to be more for the enjoyment of humans than the improvement of dogs. Breeding has also succeeded in undoing the friendliness carefully developed over tens of millennia and has produced some frighteningly aggressive breeds.

Jeffrey Masson imagined what might have happened if the tables were turned and dogs got to control human breeding for their own purposes. He suggested that we might all behave like a cross between Mahatma Gandhi – completely nonviolent – and Robin Williams – silly and playful.

The dog breeding process today is so regimented and narrowly focused that it often leads to serious health problems. A University of California / Davis research team studied the records of over 27,000 dogs over a 15-year period. This comprehensive review found that purebred dogs were more susceptible to a large number of inherited disorders than mixed-breed dogs. Findings like these have led to a movement opposed to the kind of dog breeding prevalent today. For example, veterinary scientist Lucy Asher has argued forcefully that, "No dog breed has ever been improved by the capricious and arbitrary decision that a shorter/longer/flatter/bigger/smaller/curlier 'whatever' is better. Condemning a dog to a lifetime of suffering for the sake of looks is not an improvement. It is torture" (p. 411).

Particularly disturbing is the close connection between dog breeding and the eugenics movement that arose in the 19th century and was made infamous by the Nazi party in Germany's attempts to create a master race of humans. Several founding members of the American Kennel Club, such as Executive Secretary Leon Whitney, were deeply involved in the eugenics movement and advocated selective breeding not only for dogs but for humans as well. Whitney's 1934 work *The Case for Sterilization* was one of Adolph Hitler's favorite books. Adolph sent Leon a signed letter of thanks for sending him a copy. The book advocated the sterilization of so-called "unfit" and "defective" humans to prevent them from procreating. Having spent my career advancing services, rights and acceptance for people with disabilities, this type of attitude is especially sickening to me.

After World War II, eugenics experiments on human beings were terminated and Nazi ideology was thoroughly discredited, for reasons that need no repeating. Since then, eugenicists seem to have confined their unsavory predilections to the treatment of a more defenseless population: dogs.

Breeding excesses aside, today's dogs come in a dizzying variety of shapes and sizes and perform a vast number of valuable roles in our lives. But there is one important role, perhaps the most important one, that we have yet to consider.

9

Best Friends Forever

Animals typically relate to one another as predator and prey, as mutual predators who compete or keep their distance, or they ignore one another. There are a few notable exceptions, such as the mutual assistance sharks and pilot fish provide one another. Pilot fish gain protection from sharks, and in turn they keep the sharks clean of parasites. Sharks will even open their mouths to let pilot fish clean their teeth. Oxpecker birds and hippopotami may provide similar mutual assistance.

An internet search of "unlikely animal friends" will turn up examples of what appears to be genuine friendship between individual members of different species, such as a chimpanzee and a panda. These are usually associated with some special circumstance, such as captivity or separation from an animal's customary environment or family, that motivated the animals to go beyond their usual boundaries for companionship.

Dogs and humans are the only two species that have ever become friends. Dogs generally prefer being with humans than with other dogs. In one canine psychology experiment, dogs who had spent the last eight weeks interacting with their kennel mates were given a choice to interact with their kennel mates or a human they had only known through brief interactions to feed them and clean the kennel. They chose to spend time with the human. And conversely, there are humans, like Frederick the Great of Prussia (1740 – 1786), who prefer dogs to other humans. Frederick the Great is said to be the first person to use the phrase "man's best friend" when talking about his dog.

The remarkable sensitivity of dogs to the actions and emotions of humans has been at the root of many extraordinarily close relationships between dogs and their human companions. We have seen that Richard Wagner paid attention to reactions from his dog Peps to compose some of his famous operas.

This deep bond between dogs and humans has been recognized since ancient times. Evidence can be found in ancient burial practices, because a caring burial usually reflects the respect one had in life. Anthropologists Darcy Morey and Michael Wiant published a report of carefully buried dog skeletons in what is now Illinois dated to 8,500 years ago years ago that suggests an affectionate relationship going back many millennia. Discoveries by a team of archaeologists led by University of Alberta professor Rob Losey of 14,000 year old cemeteries in the Lake Baikal region of southern Siberia also found dogs buried in the same manner as humans, and sometimes in the same graves and wearing necklaces or with other grave goods similar to those found with nearby humans. In Egypt, in the days of the pharaohs, dogs were often mummified in the same way as humans. Thousands of dog mummies have been found at a site called the "Dog Catacombs" in Saqqara, about 20 miles south of modern Cairo.

An excavation of a burial site from 12,000 – 10,000 years ago in what is now northern Israel – just west of the Golan Heights and the border with Syria – makes the ancient bond between dogs and humans strikingly clear. Twelve humans are buried together, with the bones of one woman's hand resting on the remains of a puppy. According to Rob Losey, applying the same mortuary practices to dogs as to humans is evidence that dogs in ancient times "were known as distinct persons with 'souls'" (p. 188).

The ancient Roman writer Flavius Arrian's description of his friendship with his dog Horme ("Impulse") in about the year 110 sounds as if it could have been written yesterday:

> While I am at home he remains within, by my side. When I go to the gym, he accompanies me, and while I am exercising, sits down by me. On the way back he runs before me, often looking back to see whether I had turned anywhere off the road, and as soon as he catches sight of me, showing symptoms of joy, and again trotting on before me. If I am going out on any business, he remains with my friend, and does exactly the same towards him. He is the constant companion of whoever may be sick. And if he has not seen either of us for only a short time, he jumps up repeatedly by way of salutation, and barks with joy (pp. 79-80).

Looking at the way many dogs are viewed as members of their families and the exceptional loyalty and courage shown by dogs assisting their human companions will help us appreciate more fully the special friendship between humans and dogs.

Family Members

Many people consider their dog to be a member of the family. In his *Odyssey*, Homer emphasized this family bond by having Odysseus' dog Argos be the first one in his household to recognize him when he returned home from his long travels.

An indicator of being a member of the family is that an estimated 45% of dog owners sleep with their dogs in the bed, a practice that has likely carried forward uninterrupted from paleolithic times. The French explorer Eugene Delessert journeyed to Australia in 1844 - 1845 near what is now Sydney. He kept a journal with accounts and drawings reporting his encounters with the

Aboriginal groups living there. His journal contains the following description of their family life and sleeping arrangements:

> A camp is rarely composed of more than six to eight huts, housing twenty to twenty-five individuals, men, women and children, always followed by a large number of dogs of all kinds. Their offspring are looked after by the women, who do not disdain in occasion to suckle them themselves. These dogs take up the best spots in the huts and are willingly used as pillows. They render great service to their masters by the speed with which they discover the track of certain animals (p. 102).

In his book *Cynegeticus*, the Roman writer Arrian recommended sleeping with your dog:

> There is nothing like a soft and warm bed for greyhounds, and it is best for them to sleep with men, as they become thereby affectionately attached, pleased with the contact of the human body, and as fond of their bedfellow as of their feeder. If any ailing affect the dog, the man will perceive it.... He will also know how the dog has rested (pp. 93-94).

Indications of family membership are as striking as they are numerous. As a child I was struck by the way our dog Spook, after giving birth to puppies in our home, cleaned them and presented them to us, one by one, so the rest of the family could admire how adorable they were. Perhaps the most universally appreciated indication of family membership is simply that both species enjoy one another's company. Nikita Brottman expressed the delight she found in spending time with her dog Grisby:

> Before I had Grisby, I'd heard people claim their dogs had changed their lives, but I always assumed

it was an exaggeration, a figure of speech. Since I've had Grisby, it's easy for me to see how you could sacrifice anything to spend time with your dog, or to make your dog happy. Luckily, most dogs are easy to please, and all Grisby seems to want is for the two of us to be together (p. 151).

Loyalty

The special relationship between dogs and humans is especially evident in accounts of mutual loyalty and trust. Dog loyalty is legendary. The old-fashioned dog name "Fido" means "I trust" or "I am faithful" in Latin. Before photography, in the age of portrait painting, a wedding picture would often include a dog next to the newlyweds to symbolize fidelity and devotion.

Dogs trust humans completely. Brian Hare and Vanessa Woods reported an experiment where meat was put under a cup, with a dog watching it being placed there and also smelling it. But if the experimenter pointed to a different, empty cup, the dog trusted the human and more often chose the wrong cup, against his or her own better judgment.

Sometimes the loyalty of dogs for their human companions is so deep as to be unfathomable. John Grey, a member of the Edinburgh Scotland Police Department, died in 1858 and was buried in the nearby Greyfriars churchyard. His terrier Bobby went to his master's grave and guarded it every day for the next 14 years, until Bobby died in 1872. A life-sized bronze statue of Greyfriar's Bobby stands near the spot.

14. Greyfriar's Bobby

In Tokyo, Japan near the Shibuya train station there is a similar statue to a dog named Hachiko. His "owner," Professor Ueko, took the train from there every morning to his job at the University, and Hachiko came to greet him when he returned each day on the four o'clock train. One day, Professor Ueko suffered a fatal cerebral hemorrhage as he was delivering his lectures and he never returned home. For the next ten years, Hachiko went to Shibuya station every day to meet the four o'clock train. He also has a statue at that location, looking towards the train platform.

Some commentators have tried to throw cold water on these stories, noting that Bobby and Hachiko became so well-known that people came to see them and offered them food and treats. After a while, showing up to get treats may have eclipsed their original purpose. But there must have been enough truth to the story to begin with to attract these spectators.

And loyalty goes both ways. Mackenzie King, Prime Minister of Canada during World War II, had a terrier named Pat, who was a source of stability to him through some difficult times in his personal life. Finally the day came when Pat's life was near its end, and it became clear that he would not hold on much longer.

But that happened to be the day when Prime Minister King had an important meeting scheduled with Winston Churchill and Franklin Roosevelt to plan the joint allied D-Day operation to liberate Nazi-occupied Europe.

King's solidarity with Pat was unshakeable. He postponed the meeting until the following day, hurried home and held Pat in his arms, talking and singing to him all day and all through the night, until the end. As King put it, "Morning was just beginning to break. I kissed the little fellow as he lay there, and told him of his being faithful and true, and of his having saved my soul" (quoted in Coren, p. 210). He buried Pat and then went to the meeting.

Some of the earliest known legends talk of this deep interspecies loyalty. The world's oldest epic poem, the Mahabharata, was written in Sanskrit about 2,500 years ago, based on oral versions perhaps 1,000 years earlier. Book 17 concerns the exploits of a king Yudishthira, ruler of a region of northern India bordering on today's Nepal. This king set off with his brothers and a few other companions on a journey to reach the dwelling place of the deity Indra and her fabled chariot high up in the mountains that they believed could take them to paradise. But along the difficult route, his brothers and other companions all perished, one by one, from hunger, falling accidents, or the bitter wind and cold. When his last companion was gone and Yudishthira thought he would have to attempt the rest of the journey alone, a dog appeared at his side and accompanied him. Together they made their way over jagged rocks, found food and shared it, and came to depend on one another. Finally they reached Indra. Indra congratulated Yudishthira and invited him to enter her chariot and fly to paradise. But as he and the dog approached, Indra said, "Wait, I'm afraid this dog can't come. You must leave him here. Dogs aren't allowed in paradise."

Yudishthira looked at the dog and then at Indra, and replied, "I am sorry, but I will not abandon this dog. He is my faithful companion. If it means I must abandon this dog, then I am not interested in paradise." He turned to begin the trip back down the mountain, but as he did so, the dog transformed into the god Dharma, and spoke to him. "Congratulations. You have passed the final test. By demonstrating true compassion, you have shown yourself worthy of paradise." Indra opened the chariot door, helped him in, and off they went.

Courage

Dogs have a distinguished record of military service. We have seen that armies commonly used dogs as part of an attack force since ancient times, and Flavius Arrian remarked that the soldiers who fought alongside military dogs "wept over their faithful canine companions slain in war" (p. 239).

The courage of military dogs is spellbinding. In World War I, a stray Boston terrier, Stubby, befriended the troops of the 102nd Infantry, 26th Yankee Division, who smuggled him aboard their transport ship to France and the front. The troops enjoyed his company so much that he was given his own uniform and the rank of private. Stubby took his job seriously. After experiencing a mustard gas attack and its effects, he gave himself the duty of sitting on top of the trenches and warning the troops whenever he detected the first whiff of incoming gas. This advance warning gave the troops enough time to put on their gas masks and cover their skin. Stubby performed other valiant deeds as well, including identifying a German spy dressed in an American uniform. In recognition of his outstanding service, Stubby was promoted to the rank of Sergeant. After the war he was invited to the White House and received several medals, including one presented in person by General John Pershing, commander of the American Expeditionary Force.

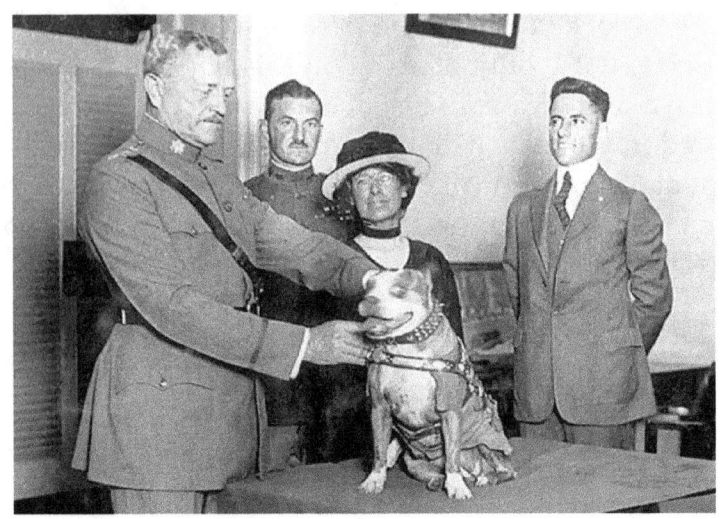

*15. Sgt. Stubby, in Uniform, Awarded Medal
by Gen. Pershing*

In World War II, Chips, a shepherd, husky and collie mix, accompanied the troops participating in the allied invasion of Italy in 1943. As the troops landed on the beach, realizing that his comrades were under fire from a machine gun nest disguised as a fishing shack, Chips charged the shack and disarmed and wounded the soldiers manning the nest, receiving wounds himself in the attack. That same night, although wounded, Chips alerted his companions to an enemy patrol that he could hear was sneaking up on the encampment under cover of darkness, and helped capture them. Chips received a Silver Star and a Purple Heart for his bravery. But this upset some people, who protested that a dog was just a tool, and had no more right to a medal than a Jeep damaged in combat. The Army held a hearing on the matter and ruled that Chips could keep his medals, but medals designed to recognize humans could no longer be awarded to dogs. The United Kingdom and many other countries still do award metals of valor to military dogs, however, and many US police forces award medals of valor to courageous K-9 dogs.

On August 7th, 2018, as this book was being prepared for publication, a new act was passed by both houses of Congress to establish a "Guardians of America's Freedom Medal" for military dogs. The bill was on it's way to receive the President's signature and become law.

A Dog's Life

A Jeep? The story of Chips highlights something important. Humans have not unequivocally embraced dogs as friends. Different people react to them differently, and the inter-species relationship has fluctuated over time.

The German shepherd Rin-Tin-Tin only play-acted participation in combat, but his experience was similar to that of Chips. He starred in 27 Hollywood films, was nominated for Best Actor at the 1929 Academy Award competition, and actually received the most votes. But the Motion Picture Academy refused to consider it, removed his name, and held a second vote.

16. Rin-Tin-Tin Gets Top Billing

Why this happened is an important story in itself; why the contributions of Chips and Rin-Tin-Tin were dismissed out of hand, why we seem to both have affectionate feelings for dogs on one hand and insist that they remain invisible and unimportant on the other. Wagner referred to Peps informally as co-author of *Lohengrin*, but only as a half-humorous remark, not a formal attribution. Sigmund Freud, likewise, mentioned Jofi's influence on psychoanalysis in a couple of letters to a friend, but not in any of his scientific works. Impressed as he was by the "undeniable solidarity" shown by dogs, he neglected to return the favor.

While Freud and Wagner kept their thoughts away from public scrutiny, Boris Levinson had the courage, or perhaps the naivete, to publically and formally credit his dog Jingles with having a healing influence on therapy patients. He was met with ridicule and scorn.

Looking back, we can see that there have been ups and downs in the status afforded to dogs in human society. The reputation of dogs has shifted along with shifts in the beliefs and values prevalent in society at a particular time and has spanned the entire distance from models of wisdom on one hand to filthy creatures in league with the devil on the other.

Teachers of Wisdom

In the ancient world, dogs were valued partly for the important life lessons they could teach us. Plato was of the opinion that their capacity to delight in small pleasures made dogs the most philosophical of all animals. A group of philosophers called the Cynics were even named after the Greek word for dog, and their philosophy was strongly influenced by their admiration for the way dogs approach life. The Cynics were not "cynical" in the sense we use that term today. They were non-conformists who believed in living as simply as possible, with a minimum of possessions. They valued speaking their minds plainly and directly, without a lot of filtering to conform to artificial social conventions. They believed in following nature, in self-sufficiency, and in freeing themselves from elements of civilization that they believed were superfluous and detrimental to virtue. They disparaged luxuries, wealth, social status and honors, and had a special disdain for pretentiousness and phoniness. They did not put their philosophy in writing, but rather lived it, as dogs do.

The most famous Cynic was Diogenes of Synope. Diogenes is said to have lived out in the open and slept in a barrel. He had only three possessions: A robe to wear, a walking stick, and a cup for drinking water from the public fountain. However, one day he observed a child drinking from the fountain simply by cupping his hands, and so, seeing that it was unnecessary, he gave his cup away. Another anecdote about Diogenes relates to a visit from Alexander the Great, who had heard of his reputation as an influential philosopher and came to see him. When Alexander asked Diogenes if there was anything he could do for him, Diogenes answered, "Yes, could you move to the side a little? You are blocking the sun."

For the Cynics, dogs were models of simplicity and dignity. Diogenes said that humans would do well to study the dog. Summing up his orientation to living, Diogenes said, "I fawn on anyone who gives me anything, bark at those who don't, and I set my teeth in rascals."

Some of the Cynic philosophy became incorporated into later philosophical systems. For example, Nietzsche viewed dogs as moral exemplars because they live close to nature. And its enduring influence can be found in a long line of back-to-nature and voluntary simplicity movements.

Demons of the Flesh

As the ancient world crumbled and monotheistic religions began to dominate Western civilization, humans' view of dogs took a decidedly downward turn. Many religious traditions have not been kind to dogs, who tended to be seen as unclean or even in league with the devil. In some traditions, life was understood as a kind of epic struggle between the spirit and the flesh; the pure and the unclean. Dogs were clearly on the flesh side: Eating with gusto, comfortable with their sexuality and bodily functions, and so on. A negative judgment about such things was considered a sign of spiritual progress.

In the *Bible*, Chapter 1 of the Book of Genesis says that we humans were given dominion, or command, over all other animals, which seemed to give humans license to treat them as well or as poorly as we wished. And dogs were listed among the negative influences on people in the New Testament book of the Apocalypse (also called Revelation):

> Blessed are those who wash their garments in the blood of the Lamb; so they will have access to the tree which gives life, and find their way through the gates of the city. No room there for prowling dogs, for sorcerers and wantons and murderers and idolators, for anyone who loves falsehood... (22: 14-15).

As modern philosophical systems developed, philosophers placed dogs among the lower animals because they did not reason and use language the way humans do. Rene Descartes considered dogs as automatons with no soul, and Immanuel Kant considered them as "brutes" with no rights.

With the advent of modern science and medicine, mention of dogs was almost exclusively in the context of warning of the danger of disease and the menace to public health they were thought to pose. With the advent of scientific psychology, behaviorists criticized anyone who ascribed characteristics such as consciousness or emotions to dogs as hopelessly sentimental. As the twentieth century got underway, Freud provided a summary of the situation as he saw it:

> In the course of his development towards culture man acquired a dominating position over his fellow-creatures in the animal kingdom. Not content with this supremacy, however, he began to place a gulf between his nature and theirs. He denied the possession of reason to them, and to himself he attributed an immortal soul, and made claims to a divine descent which permitted him to annihilate the bond of community between him and the animal kingdom (p. 137).

The "annihilation" that Freud wrote about meant that dogs were rendered practically invisible, and their behavior was dismissed as simplistic and mechanical. Use of dog commands like "Come" and "Stay" are a relic of this mechanical view. And any mention of the contributions of dogs to human progress – valor in combat, co-authoring operas, keeping decision-makers calm during international crises, starring in Hollywood films, helping heal therapy patients, and so on – was strictly forbidden by the mores of the time. Freud himself should be considered a co-conspirator in this annihilation, because in his extensive writings and lectures on the methods and results of psychoanalysis he made no mention of his dog Jofi, even though he was fully aware of Jofi's contribution. The therapeutic role of dogs had to be rediscovered by Boris Levinson, and even then it came close to being completely ignored.

David Hagner, Ph.D.

Good Dog

Starting slowly but picking up speed around the second half of the twentieth century, the status of dogs was once again on the rise. This was the era of Levinson's pioneering work. One plausible theory is that our modern system of dog licensing and rabies vaccination is partly responsible for a cleaner image of dogs.

The reputation of dogs also benefitted from the fact that science had progressed on a number of fronts. We learned of the previously unappreciated cognitive abilities of many animals, such as tool use by chimpanzees and the communication ability of dolphins, and psychological theory had begun to add new cognitive perspectives as alternatives to simple behaviorism. These developments helped elevate our view of dogs once again to the role of our best friends.

Their status has even risen among contemporary philosophers. Heather Douglas, professor of Philosophy at the University of Tennessee, reminds us that although humans are rational animals, we tend to overemphasize the rational half. She believes that an important lesson we can learn from dogs is how to come in closer contact with and be more welcoming of our animal selves. Another contemporary philosopher, Randall Auxier at Southern Illinois University, noted that we can better appreciate the philosophical approach known as radical empiricism from observing how dogs approach their environment. For them, the world of sense experiences is so intensely absorbing that it demands complete attention and detailed investigation.

The relationship between humans and dogs has always been a two-way street. Because dogs are so sensitive to nuances of human behavior, our attitude towards them is reflected back in the way they relate to us. Our style of interaction affects how they respond. The story of St. Patrick is a striking example. As a boy,

Patrick was a caretaker to Irish wolfhounds being transported by ship to mainland Europe for use as hunting dogs. He learned to control spirited dogs who disliked sea travel by showing them calmness, attention to their feelings, and respect. As an adult, he became a priest and set out to convert Ireland to Christianity. When Patrick landed with his band of missionaries, the local Druids, led by chief Dichu and his ferocious Irish wolfhound Luath, prepared to drive them away. Dichu signaled Luath to attack, but as Luath lunged forward, Patrick knelt down and extended his hands. Luath halted, then quietly approached and nuzzled Patrick's hand. Deeply impressed, Dichu called off the attack and asked for instruction in the new religion.

Since the attitude and behavior of a human has a major influence on the behavior of a dog, when the human isn't a good companion, the dog can't be a good dog. If we see them as mindless brutes, that is how they will act. How we relate to a dog is not a matter of technique, and it can't be faked. Ultimately, it is a reflection of how we view our partner species and their place in our families and communities.

10

Is a Dog a Person?

We have seen that in ancient times dogs were sometimes buried in the same manner as and sometimes together with humans, and that this has been interpreted as suggesting that dogs "were known as distinct persons with 'souls'". There is also some historical evidence of dogs being regarded as persons. For example, in the 13th century a greyhound credited with saving a sleeping baby from being bitten by a poisonous snake was venerated as a saint – Saint Guinefort – in the Burgundy region of France, although never officially declared a saint. (An interesting sideline to this story is that it was common, and not considered neglectful, for humans to leave their babies in the care of a dog.)

Dogs have also been tried and punished for committing crimes, something it only makes sense to do to persons. Following the infamous 1619 Salem witch trials, two dogs were executed along with 19 women. Is a dog a person?

Self-Awareness

For a behaviorist, a dog's actions are governed by nothing more than instinct and conditioning. Attributing any more than this to a dog is considered anthropomorphism – giving human qualities to creatures that don't have them.

If dogs are simply mindless mechanisms they cannot be persons. To be a person would seem to require additional mental capacity, such as a significant level of cognitive ability and self-awareness.

It seems clear that dogs have emotions, preferences and interests, fears, disappointments and joys, and they are capable of forming and using concepts on at least a rudimentary level. David DeGrazia, a philosophy professor at Georgetown University interested in animal cognition, noted that:

> I believe there is food in the kitchen. But can my dog...entertain such propositions? To do so, he would seem to need concepts. Does he really have the concepts of food, eating, kitchen, and so on? Presumably he doesn't have our concepts of food as nourishing, eating as applicable to all creatures with mouths, and kitchens as rooms used for cooking. But perhaps he has his own concepts that pick out these items even if the conceptual scaffolding differs from that of our concepts (2002, p. 204).

Dogs also initiate actions to pursue goals and make choices and plans based on their preferences. This seems to imply a certain level of self-awareness. DeGrazia believes there is ample evidence that dogs are self-aware and that they possess a particularly acute social self-awareness. They:

> Display a keen awareness of how they fit into social groups, the expectations for individuals in their social positions, who has behaved toward them as allies and who as enemies, what they "owe" to particular individuals based on past interactions, and the like. All of this requires some type of social self-awareness (2009, p. 114).

There is even some evidence, as we saw with a study by Brigit Stetina and her colleagues at the University of Vienna, that observing a dog's behavior can help us humans respond better to the emotions of other people. Despite this evidence, many people find it difficult to let go of a longstanding tradition of skepticism about dogs having minds. Three responses can be offered to the skeptic.

Immediate Recognition

How do you know that other humans have minds? How do they know that you have a mind? Such questions almost seem silly.

It has become popular in recent years to say that humans have a "theory of mind." But despite its popularity, this way of thinking is surely mistaken. Philosopher Ludwig Wittgenstein pointed out the mistake in advance, as it were, three decades before the "theory of mind" was put forward. He uses the word "soul" instead of "mind," but his argument holds up just the same.

> Suppose I say of a friend, "He isn't an automaton." What information is conveyed by this, and to whom would it be information? To a human being who meets him in ordinary circumstances? What information could it give him? "I believe that he is not an automaton"...makes no sense. My attitude towards him is an attitude towards a soul. I am not of the opinion that he has a soul (p. 178).

We don't infer that other humans have minds. We don't need a theory. We immediately recognize another mind. When my baby grandson Greyson drops a toy and looks at me, I can tell he is hoping I can help get it back. I reach down and get the toy. Two minds communicate directly and wordlessly. When our family dog Poco pushes a bone under a chair by mistake, he looks at me, and I can tell he is hoping I can help solve the problem. I stick my arm under the chair and get the bone. Two minds communicate directly and wordlessly. Relating to a dog *is* relating to another mind.

The Intentional Stance

The second response is drawn from philosopher Daniel Dennett's proposal that while simple actions – stopping your car at a red light, for example – may be open to a mechanistic or conditioning-based explanation, it would be too cumbersome, even if theoretically possible, to explain complex actions – going shopping, for example – in a mechanistic way. To talk about these actions, it is easier and more natural to refer to a shopper's intentions, goals, desires, beliefs, and so on. Intentional descriptions can be thought of as shorthand descriptions of complex behavior.

A mechanistic understanding of dog behavior is similarly unwieldy. We naturally talk of them having intentions, and therefore having minds.

Self-fulfilling Prophesies

A related consideration is that our beliefs can be self-fulfilling prophesies. For example, do you believe that people are fundamentally good? Or bad? How you act towards people affects them, and so whatever beliefs you have about them are rendered more true because of your beliefs. The impact of belief may be small, but we can see it in amplified form in novels like *Don Quixote* by Cervantes and its musical adaptation *Man of La Mancha*. Don Quixote's belief that Dulcinea, a barmaid with loose morals, was a virtuous princess changed her life. Similarly, by treating dogs as if they have emotions, beliefs, goals, and so on, we influence them to develop further in this direction than they otherwise would.

Sir Walter Scott talked to his dog Camp in the same sentences he would use with anyone else, not because he had hard evidence that Camp understood language thoroughly, but because he thought Camp and his other dogs deserved that degree of respect, as his walking companions, and could most likely pick up enough of what he said to make this worthwhile. And when Washington Irving came for a visit, he wrote in his letters back home that "... there appears to be a vast deal of rationality that these faithful attendants of man derived from their close intimacy with him" (quoted in Coren, p. 86). In other words, Scott's approach elevated his dogs' understanding beyond what it would otherwise have been.

An accusation of anthropomorphism is justified, though, in situations where a human goes far beyond observational evidence and imagines that they can tell that the dog likes the color of his new collar, for example, or is upset that nobody remembered her birthday. Psychoanalyst Mikita Brottman pointed out that interpretations like this of a dog's actions or emotions says more about the human's hopes, fears, and attitudes than the dog's. Some humans use dogs as an indirect way to give voice to complaints, confessions, and feelings they are reluctant to express directly. Projecting them onto the dog provides an outlet for the human but is unfair to the dog.

So if we grant that dogs have mental states, self-awareness, and so on, does this mean that they are persons? The problem with such a position is that we keep finding out how much cognitive ability all sorts of creatures have. Many primates, for example, use tools and can learn language. Birds in the corvid family (ravens, crows, magpies and jays) have demonstrated surprisingly sophisticated problem-solving skills, and some parrots can make logical inferences and can even grasp the concept of zero, something human mathematicians struggled over for millennia. Dolphins and whales seem to have rich interpersonal communication systems. Even cephalopods (e.g. octopi and squid) have been found to be surprisingly intelligent. So are they all persons? This seems to be going off the deep end.

Moral Responsibility

We might consider restricting the term "person" to a being with the ability to self-consciously follow moral rules, make moral judgments, and take responsibility for one's behavior. At first glance, this is a tall order that would seem to leave dogs out. But there are complexities to consider.

When dogs do something wrong, it seems a stretch to think that they interpret their behavior as disobeying a moral rule. Even if they look guilty, we might see this as sort of an act that they put on to get back in our good graces, rather than a real recognition of the moral weight of the action. But don't humans sometimes do that too?

On the other hand, there are occasions when it seems to me that Poco's behavior can be described to some degree as acting morally. He can tell, as soon as we go outdoors, whether I am headed for the chicken house or the wood pile, and he runs ahead with a sprightly step and a merry demeanor to lead the way to where I am going. Poco seems proud of his ability to anticipate the destination, and under certain circumstances – such as if I became lost, or there was a dangerous animal on the path – his behavior would be very useful. The behavior is probably instinctive; there is no point in denying that dogs do a lot of things instinctively. But what about the sprightly step and merry demeanor? This particular attitude seems reserved for situations where Poco recognizes that he can be of service by leading the way. It looks for all the world like he knows what his role is and that he is carrying it out properly. That comes close, at least, to saying that he is doing something because he knows it's the right thing for him to do.

A dog is undoubtedly not a moral being in the same full sense as a human. Dogs aren't human. Their ability to use concepts is limited, and their sense of time is confined more to the present.

Satisfying an urge of the moment has more weight for them than for us, and considering long-term consequences has less weight for them than for us. Their lives are very different. But that does not in itself mean that dogs never act morally or never deliberately obey rules that they have learned are important for them to follow. Only prejudice would lead one to say that dogs are not persons because they are not humans.

An argument against considering dogs as moral beings is that they are pretty selfish. When a dog licks your face, it might be to give you a kiss, or the dog might just be checking out what you have been eating lately. Morality, on the other hand, seems to call for a healthy dose of altruism.

But several philosophers, including Friedrich Nietzsche, held the view that what we call altruism is often a disguised form of selfishness. And Nikita Brottman considered it refreshing that dogs can be guilt-free about being selfish, adding, "Doesn't our admiration for dogs include a bit of envy that part of their charm is their ability to pull off unabashed selfishness without even a tinge of guilt?" (p. 70).

Dogs do seem to have a basic understanding of fairness. In one psychological experiment, pairs of dogs played a game of "give me your paw" for rewards, sitting next to one another. One was given a better reward (a piece of sausage) than the other (a piece of bread). The dog with the smaller reward stopped playing the game sooner than the other dog. This dog went on strike because the reward wasn't equitable.

A fair conclusion might be that glimmers of morality seem to be found in dog behavior, but that adopting the high bar of fully moral behavior probably leaves them out of the running as beings we should regard as persons. But there is a problem with setting the bar this high. Fully moral behavior is also lacking in human infants and also in some people with significant developmental or psychiatric disabilities. We do not on that account consider them to be non-persons.

So the criterion of self-awareness seems too soft, and the criterion of full moral responsibility seems too hard. Is there a criterion for being a person that is in the just right Goldilocks zone?

The Moral Sentiment

Sharon Krause, professor of political science at Brown University, proposed an idea drawn from the philosophers of the Scottish Enlightenment. These philosophers grounded morality in what they called the "moral sentiment." One of them, Adam Smith, best known for his economic theories, also wrote a book called *The Theory of The Moral Sentiment*. This theory may provide us with a criterion for personhood that will help us answer our question.

The moral sentiment is a feeling similar to what we call empathy – the ability to resonate with and identify with the pleasures and pains of others. This feeling arises as we experience, through our powers of imagination and perspective-taking, the sentiments of others we are in contact with. As we begin to sense what someone else is feeling, we are pulled to some extent into sharing that feeling. We cringe a little when they are hurt and brighten up when they hear good news. Such interpersonal communication of feeling comes naturally to us.

Recent neuropsychological research has even localized particular regions of the brain involved in the recognition of emotions in others. Individuals less able to feel empathy for others exhibit less activity in these regions.

The moral sentiment provides us with a criterion of personhood. A person is a member of the community of beings who can feel what others feel and share each others' sentiments. This connection is what makes complex social interactions possible and serves as the foundation for morality.

There is some evidence that dogs have a moral sentiment. Experiments have shown that they engage in consolation behavior with other dogs. When they watch two dogs fighting and one wins while the other loses, they initiate contact more often with the loser, apparently drawn to the whimpering, and console them.

It also seems clear that dogs respond to what humans are feeling. We saw in Chapter 1 that in one therapy dog effectiveness study, a dog assisting children who were experiencing severe pain was observed seeming to take on the pain of a child, and had to receive massages and other measures to calm down.

At the very least, some dogs some of the time display a moral sentiment. Based on this criterion, dogs at least come close to being creatures we should regard as persons. We recognize some responsibility toward them, some obligations as part of our solidarity with them. A reasonable position might be to recognize dogs as quasi-persons or honorary persons. The medieval philosopher Thomas Aquinas apparently held a view like this. His position, as summarized by Fordham University's Thomist scholar W. Norris Clarke, was that animals possessing a certain amount of ability to initiate actions and make choices share a limited or partial participation in the self-conscious freedom that characterizes human persons.

A Dog's View of Humans

How do dogs view their relationship with us? They most likely realize that humans are very different kinds of creatures than themselves. When mothers and their babies gaze at each other, it often creates a positive oxytocin feedback loop for both mother and baby. This same feedback loop occurs between dogs and humans. Some researchers have concluded from this that the attachment of dogs to their "owners" is similar to the attachment of babies to their mothers. But that does not mean that the mother/child relationship is a model for human/dog relationships. Some humans treat dogs as children to some extent, but it is doubtful that dogs view humans as their mothers.

Another theory that was current for a while but seems to have waned in recent years is that dogs relate to humans as so-called "alpha dogs." They think of the family they live with as a pack, and figure out relationships the way wolves do within a pack. They identify one of the humans as the member of the pack who is in charge, and obey that person. According to this theory, if none of the humans establish themselves as alpha dogs by exercising authoritarian control, dogs will come to think that the position is vacant, and that perhaps they should be the alpha dog, and then they will start trying to run the household.

There is little evidence that this is the case. Elyssa Payne, professor of Veterinary Science at the University of Sydney, noted that "Dogs do not generally view humans as surrogate dogs; thus, social dominance may not apply in the dog-human dyad" (p. 74). Interestingly, in dog packs today that roam freely, composed of dogs with long ancestries of human contact – sometimes incorrectly called feral dogs – there is no traditional alpha dog. The leaders are not the most physically dominant members, and hierarchies are more fluid. Their wolf-like understanding of pack organization has apparently weakened.

Humans often refer to themselves as the "companions" of dogs, and Miho Nagasawa, animal scientist at Azabu University in Japan, offered the suggestion that dogs may view humans as their "cool friends" (p. 335). But this implies a level of equality that doesn't seem realistic, and I doubt that dogs themselves would accept it. They know very well that we call the shots.

It would be helpful to find a substitute for the word "owner". When I must use the word, I put it between quotation marks. We certainly don't want to think of our relationship with our dog as like our relationship with our Jeep. "Master" seems hardly better. Dog owners are legally referred to as "guardians" in some American communities, but this covers only the legalistic aspects of the relationship. What about "stewards"? Or, if you liken the relationship more to the feudal system than to slavery, feel free to call yourself the dog's "lord."

The simple fact is that our relationship with dogs is unique. It is futile to search for a comparable relationship that will help clarify it. The co-evolution of our two species may wind up being a one-time occurrence on our planet. The wisest course might be to simply and wordlessly enjoy it, as dogs do, and consider the mystery of relating to a very different species as part of the enjoyment.

Dogs have some impressive abilities, including cognitive abilities, but it is not fair to compare these to humans. When we use words like "mind" and "concept," we have to realize that there is a gulf across species in how to apply such terms. Words forged in the context of human-to-human interactions can't apply to another species in a straightforward way. There is no point in asking, for example, "Can a dog really love a human?" Some people don't mind saying that their relationship with their dog is one of love. Others reserve "love" for human relationships. With no frame of reference to go by, and no precedent to consult, either viewpoint seems valid.

Dogs will never see things in exactly the way we wish they did. For example, they can't figure out the implications of our having an upright posture. The Centers for Disease Control estimate that more than 85,000 Americans are injured each year by tripping over their dogs. And it seems that no amount of evidence will ever convince dogs to give up the belief that the faster they eat, the more food they might get. We have to accept that to some degree their perspective will always be different. For all we know, dogs might engage in what philosopher Wendy Lee has called "poochomorphism" (p. 261), such as thinking to themselves "Look how much this human likes tugging on a stuffed toy!" Neither of us will ever fully understand the other.

But that doesn't matter. Dogs are our ambassadors to the world of naturalness, simplicity, and unfiltered joy. Curled up on a luxurious pillow, shamelessly licking their private parts, they are sentries at the gate between wildness and civilization, guardians of the world of the here and now.

Part of our amazing bond with them is the way it summons us to stretch beyond our ordinary conceptual categories and appreciate a being that experiences things from a very different perspective. To be a friend to a dog is to participate in a friendship so deep and so profound that it transcends species boundaries. That is what matters.

CONCLUSION

When Boris Levinson made a conference presentation in the early 1960s suggesting that dogs could serve as co-therapists for children with behavioral difficulties, his ideas were met with derision. Members of the audience shouted out wisecrack comments like "How much does the dog charge?" I propose that we take this question seriously. Let's draw up an invoice, based on what we know about dogs, itemizing what they charge for their services.

- Dogs need a comfortable home and a caring family. They love being part of a social group, and dislike spending long periods of time alone. They experience separation anxiety. If a dog left alone too long scratches the door or gets into other mischief, the one with the problem is the human responsible for that.

- Dogs know what we're having for dinner, and consider it a great honor – as did the proto-dogs before them, the wolf-dogs before them, the dog-wolves before them, and those first friendly, curious and courageous wolves before them who showed up at dinner time – to receive a few pieces of what we're cooking, perhaps mixed in with commercial "dog food." For spicy foods, pieces can be reserved for the dog before serious spices are added.

- Dogs need substantial amounts of time outdoors and opportunities to sniff the environment and occasionally follow a smell track to see where it goes. And once in a while dogs need to run fast and far and participate in some roughhouse play.

- Most dogs appreciate opportunities to interact with other dogs and receive some "peer support."

17. Friends Playing at Dog Park

Poco's friend was an old dog named Spencer who lived next door. I'm not sure if Spencer really liked Poco or just came over to poop in our yard. But Poco thought Spencer was awesome. He passed away almost a year ago. Poco still looks out the window every morning to see if Spencer is coming over.

- Dogs have active brains that need stimulation, interest and variety. They like to have a purpose or task to work on. When they can't help hunt or herd, they can accompany us on a long walk or hike. What we think of as mere enjoyment, our dog considers a serious mission. And indoors, everyday tasks can be constructed. On laundry day, Poco's job is to pick out a dirty sock and bring it down to the laundry. And Poco likes to shred things, so when I need paper shredded, I ball it up and throw it to "Poco's Secure Shredding Service – Guaranteed Torn to Bits and Blurred with Saliva," and he goes to work.

- According to Aristotle, a friend is someone you appreciate for their virtues. We should appreciate and praise dogs, and not for their looks alone, but also for their strength, speed, loyalty, alertness, and many other virtues.

- The language we use in relation to dogs should reflect our values. Using the expression "dog...who" rather than "dog...that" honors their quasi-personhood (although my word processing program flags this as incorrect). And dogs ask for food, they don't "beg". Why would they want charity instead of their fair share of the wealth they helped create? And we can talk to dogs using ordinary language rather than special dog commands, a residue of sterile behaviorism. Downgrading dogs leads to the kind of disparaging comments people made about Boris Levinson and Jingles and their work together.

Along with the legitimate charge for their services, dogs also have doggie responsibilities: No peeing or pooping in the house; if you roll in smelly stuff, accept that you will get a bath; no jumping up on people uninvited; and no biting unless you are asked to.

The dog is an extension of us, and we are an extension of the dog. Dogs would have never developed many of their abilities if it were not for their close association with us, and the same is true for humans. Our development, and civilization itself, was built in part on the foundation of our partnership with them. For tens of thousands of years they have responded to our emotions and actions in ways that help us relax, enjoy the present moment, and more deeply understand ourselves. And when we experience difficulties, we can count on dogs to help us heal and grow. Without our relationship with dogs we would be less fully human.

Their solidarity with us is undeniable. In return, we owe it to them to remember how special they are, to make sure a few simple, straightforward needs are met, and to befriend them in the same spirit of undeniable solidarity.

SOURCES

Chapter 1

Barak, Y, Savorai, O., Mavashev, S., & Beni, A. (2001). Animal-assisted therapy for elderly schizophrenic patients: A one-year controlled trial. *The American Journal of Geriatric Psychiatry, 9,* 439-442.

Barker, R., Kniseley, J., Barker, S., Cobb, R., & Schubert, C. (2012). Preliminary investigation of employees' dog presence on stress and organizational perceptions. *International Journal of Workplace Health Management, 5,* 15-30.

Berry, A., Borgi, M., Terranova, L., Chiarotti, F., Alleva, E. & Cirulli, F. (2012). Developing effective animal-assisted intervention programs involving visiting dogs for institutionalized geriatric patients: A pilot study. *Psychogeriatrics, 12,* 143-150.

Berry, A., Borgi, M., Franca, N., Alleva, E., & Cirulli, F. (2013). Use of assistance and therapy dogs for children with autism spectrum disorders: A critical review of the current evidence. *Journal of Alternative and Complementary Medicine, 19* (2), 73-80.

Braun, C., Stangler, T., Narveson, J., & Pettingill, S. (2009). Animal-assisted therapy as a pain relief intervention for children. *Complementary Therapies in Clinical Practice, 15,* 105-109.

Brottman, M. (2014). *The great Grisby: Two thousand years of literary, royal, philosophical, and artistic dog lovers and their exceptional animals.* New York NY: Harper Collins

Burch, M. (2003). Wanted: Animal volunteers. New York NY: Wiley.

Burrows, K., Adams, C., & Spiers, J. (2008). Sentinels of safety: Service dogs ensure safety and enhance freedom and well-being for families with autistic children. *Qualitative Health Research, 18,* 1642-1649.

Collins, A. (2014). *Man's best hero: True stories of great American dogs.* Nashville TN: Abington Press.

Coren, S. (2002). *The pawprints of history.* New York NY: Simon & Schuster.

Coren, S. (2013). How therapy dogs almost never came to exist. *Psychology Today,* Canine Corner blog, Feb 11.

Daltry, R. & Mehr, K. (2015). Therapy dogs on campus: Recommendations for counseling center outreach. *Journal of College Student Psychotherapy, 29,* 72-78.

Dansey, W. & Arrian, F. (1831/2010). *Arrian on coursing: The Cynegeticus of the Younger Xenophon, translated from the Greek with classical and practical annotations and a brief sketch of the life and writings of the author.* LaVergne TN, BiblioLife.

Dietz, T., Davis, D., & Pennings, J. (2012). Evaluating animal-assisted therapy in group treatment for child sexual abuse. *Journal of Child Sexual Abuse, 21,* 665-683.

Esteves, S., & Stokes, T. (2008). Social effects of a dog's presence on children with disabilities. *Anthrozoos, 21* (1), 5-15.

Freud, E. (Ed.) (1960). *Letters of Sigmund Freud*. New York NY: Basic Books.

Friesen, L. (2010). Exploring animal-assisted programs with children in school and therapeutic contexts. *Early Childhood Education Journal, 37,* 261-267.

Fry-Johnson, Y., Powell, S. & Winokur, D. (2009). Service dogs: Facilitating the abilities of children with intellectual or behavioral disabilities. *International Journal of Child and Adolescent Health, 2,* 417-421.

Funahashi, A., Gruebler, A., Aoki, T., Kadone, H., & Suzuki, K. (2014). The smiles of a child with autism spectrum disorder during an animal-assisted activity may facilitate positive social behaviors: Quantitative analysis with a smile-detecting interface. *Journal of Autism and Developmental Disorders, 44,* 6854-693.

Fung, S., & Leung, A. (2014). Pilot study investigating the role of therapy dogs in facilitating social interaction among children with autism. *Journal of Contemporary Psychotherapy, 44,* 253- 262.

Gee, N., Belcher, J., Grabski, J., DeJesus, M. & Riley, W. (2012). The presence of a therapy dog results in improved object recognition performance in preschool children. *Anthrozoos, 25,* 289-300.

Gonzalez-Ramirez, M., Ortiz-Jimenez, X., & Landero-Hernandez, R. (2013). Cognitive-behavioral therapy and animal-assisted therapy: Stress management for adults. *Alternative and Complementary Therapies, 19,* 270-275.

Grigore, A., & Rusu, A. (2014). Interaction with a therapy dog enhances the effects of social story method in autistic children. *Society and Animals, 22,* 241-261.

Groomes, D., Clemons, A., Hulme, S., Kort, K. & Mesibov, G. (2014). Utilizing assistive dogs in integrated employment settings: Multidisciplinary elements to consider for individuals with ASD. *Journal of Vocational Rehabilitation, 40,* 165-173.

Hare, B. & Woods, V. (2013). *The genius of dogs: How dogs are smarter than you think.* New York NY: Penguin.

Harper, C., Dong, Y., Thornhill, T., Wright, J., Ready, J., Brick, G., & Dyer, G. (2015). Can therapy dogs improve pain and satisfaction after total joint arthroplasty? A randomized controlled trial. *Clinical Orthopaedics and Related Research, 437,* 372-379.

Havey, J., Vlasses, F., Vlasses, P., Ludwig-Beymer, P., & Hackbarth, D. (2014). The effect of animal-assisted therapy on pain medication use after joint replacement. *Anthrozoos, 27,* 361-369.

Hoffmann, A., Lee, A., Wertenauer, F., Ricken, R., Jansen, J., Gallinat, J. et al. (2009). Dog-assisted intervention significantly reduces anxiety in hospitalized patients with major depression. *European Journal of Integrative Medicine, 1,* 145-148.

Hunt, M. & Chizkov, R. (2014). Are therapy dogs like Xanax? Does animal-assisted therapy impact processes relevant to cognitive behavioral psychotherapy? *Anthrozoös, 27,* 457-469.

Johnson, C. (2006). *The Mayflower and her passengers.* Philadelphia PA: Xlibris.

Kumasaka, T., Masu, H., Kataoka, M., & Numao, A. (2012). Physiological responses by college students to a dog and a cat: Implications for changes in patient mood through animal-assisted activities in a palliative care unit. *International Medical Journal, 19,* 373-377.

Le Roux, M., & Kemp, R. (2009). Effect of a companion dog on depression and anxiety levels of elderly residents in a long-term care facility. Psychogeriatrics, 9 (1), 23-26.

Marcus, D., Bernstein, C., Constantin, J., Kunkel, F., Breuer, P., & Hanlon, R. (2012). Animal-assisted therapy at an outpatient pain management clinic. *Pain Medicine, 13*, 45-57.

Marcus, D., Blazek-O'Neill, B., & Kopar, J. (2014). Symptom reduction identified after offering animal-assisted activity at a cancer infusion center. *American Journal of Hospice & Palliative Medicine, 31*, 420-421.

Mosselo, E., Ridolfi, A., Melo, A., Lorenzini, G., Mugnasi, G., Piccini, C., Barone, D., et al. (2011). Animal-assisted activity and emotional status of patients with Alzheimer's disease in day care. *International Psychogeriatrics, 23*, 889-905.

Nathans-Barel, I., Feldmanc, P., Berger, B., Modaic, I., & Silvera, H. (2005). Animal-assisted therapy ameliorates anhedonia in schizophrenia patients: A controlled pilot study. *Psychotherapy and Psychosomatics 74*, 31-36.

Newton, I. (1726/1999). *The Principia: Mathematical Principles of Natural Philosophy.* I B. Cohen & A. Whitman, translators. Berkeley CA: University of California Press.

Ng, Z., Pierce, B., Otto, C., Buechner-Maxwell, V., Siracusa, C., & Werre, S. (2014). The effect of dog-human interaction on cortisol and behavior in registered animal-assisted activity dogs. *Applied Animal Behaviour Science, 159* (10), 69-81.

Payne, E., Bennett, P., & McGreevy, P. (2015). Current perspectives on attachment and bonding in the dog-human dyad. *Psychology Research and Behavior Management, 8*, 71-79.

Rogers, C. (1951). Client centered therapy: Current practice, implications, and theory. Boston MA: Houghton Mifflin.

Rogers, C. (1961). *On becoming a person*. Boston MA: Houghton Mifflin.

Schuck,. S., Emmerson, N., Fine, A., & Lakes, K. (2015). Canine-assisted therapy for children with ADHD: Preliminary findings from the Positive Assertive Cooperative Kids study. *Journal of Attention Disorders, 19*, 125-137.

Solomon, O. (2010). What a dog can do: Children with autism and therapy dogs in social interaction. **Ethos. 38** (1), 143-166).

Somerville, J., Kruglikova, Y., Robertson, R., Hanson, L., & MacLin, O. (2008). Physiological responses by college students to a dog and a cat: Implications for pet therapy. *North American Journal of Psychology, 10*, 519-528.

Stetina, B., Turner, K., Burger, E., Glenk, L., McElheney, J. Handlos, U., & Kothgassner, O. (2011). Learning emotion recognition from canines? Two for the road. Journal of *Veterinary Behavior: Clinical Applications and Research, 6*, 108-114.

Traverse, C., Perkins, J., Rand, J., Bartlett, H., & Morton, J. (2013). An evaluation of dog-assisted therapy for residents of aged care facilities with dementia. *Anthrozoos, 26*, 213-225.

Viau, R., Arsenault-Lapierre, G., Fecteau, S., Champagne, N., Walker, C., & Lupien, S. (2012). Effect of service dogs on salivary cortisol secretion in autistic children. *Journal of Psychoneuroendocrinology 35*, 1187-1193.

Villalta-Gill, V., Gonzalez, N., Domenec, E., Escanilla, A., Asensio, M. Esteban, M. Ochoa, S., et al. (2009). Dog-assisted therapy in the treatment of chronic schizophrenia inpatients. *Anthrozoos, 22*, 149-159.

White, J., Quinn, M., Garland, S., Dirkse, D., Wiebe, P., Hermann, M., & Carlson, L. (2015). Animal-assisted therapy and counseling support for women with breast cancer: An exploration of patients' perceptions. *Integrative Cancer Therapies, 14*, 460-467.

Yount, R., Ritchie, E., Laurent, M., Chumley, P., & Olmert, M. (2013). The role of service dog training in the treatment of combat-related PTSD. *Psychiatric Annals, 43*, 292-295.

Zents, C., Fisk, A., & Lauback, C. (2015). *PAWS for Intervention: A Qualitative Analysis of Positive Psychological and Academic Outcomes for Students.* Annual Conference, NY State Association of School Psychologists, Albany NY, February.

Chapter 2

Bernier, A., Beauchamp, M., Bouvette-Turcot, A., Carlson, S. & Carrier, J. (2013). Sleep and cognition in preschool years: Specific links to executive functioning. *Child Development, 84,* 1542-1553.

Blair, C. & Diamond, A. (2008). Biological processes in prevention and intervention: The promotion of self-regulation as a means of preventing school failure. *Developmental Psychopathology 20,* 899–911.

Blair, J., Mitchell, D., & Blair, K. (2005). The psychopath: Emotion and the brain. Malden MA: Blackwell.

Checa, P. & Rueda, M. (2011). Behavioral and brain measures of executive attention and school competence in late childhood. *Developmental Neuropsychology, 36,* 1018–1032.

D'Errico, F., Henshilwood, C., Lawson, G., Vanhaeren, M., Tillier, A., Soressi, M., Bresson, F., et al. (2003). Archaeological evidence for the emergence of language, symbolism, and music: An alternative multidisciplinary perspective. *Journal of World Prehistory, 17,* 1 – 70.

Dyer, C. (2013) The Aboriginal people in Sydney as seen by Eugene Delessert, December 1844 to August 1845. *Aboriginal History, 37,* 93 - 110.

Gazzaniga, M. (2008). *Human: The science behind what makes us unique.* NY: Harper-Collins.

Gee, H. (2013). *The accidental species: Misunderstandings of human evolution.* Chicago IL: Chicago Univ. Press.

Groves, C. (1999). The advantages and disadvantages of being domesticated. *Perspectives on Human Biology, 4* (1), 1-12.

Hare, R. (1999). *Without conscience: The disturbing world of the psychopaths among us.* New York: NY: Guilford Press.

Hare, B. & Woods, V. (2013). *The genius of dogs: How dogs are smarter than you think.* New York NY: Penguin.

Harris, S. (2010). *The moral landscape: How science can determine human values.* New York: Free Press.

Hart, D., & Sussman, P. (2008). *Man the hunted: Primates, predators and human evolution.* Boulder CO: Westview Press.

Henshilwood, C., d'Errico, F., Vanhaeren, M., van Niekerk, K., & Jacobs, Z. (2004). Middle stone age shell beads from South Africa. *Science, 304,* 404.

Hitchcock, D. (2015). *Tools of the stone age.* Retrieved from http://donsmaps.com/makingflinttools.html

Hrdy, S. (2009). *Mothers and others: The evolutionary origins of mutual understanding.* Harvard Univ. Press.

Martins, A., Faisca, L., Esteves, F., Muresan, A. & Reis, A. (2012). Atypical moral judgment following traumatic brain injury. *Judgment and Decision Making, 7,* 478-487.

Mendez, M. (2009). The neurobiology of moral behavior: Review and neuropsychiatric implications. *CNS Spectrum, 14,* 698-620.

Newby, J. (1997). *The pact for survival: Humans and their animal companions.* Sydney, AU: ABC Books.

Paxton, D. (2000a). The case for a naturalistic perspective. *Anthrozoos, 13,* 5-8.

Paxton, D. (2000b). A case for a naturalistic perspective: Response to Lawrence and Beckoff. *Anthrozoos, 13,* 13-14.

Roberts, R. & Bird, M. (2012). Evolutionary anthropology: Homo "incendius". *Nature, 485,* 586-587.

Rueda, M., Checa, P., & Rothbart, M. (2010). Contributions of attentional control to social emotional and academic development. *Early Education and Development, 21,* 744–764.

Shipman, P. (2015). *The invaders: How humans and their dogs drove Neanderthals to extinction.* Cambridge MA: Harvard University Press.

Stringer, C. (2012). *Lone survivors: How we came to be the only humans on earth.* NY: Henry Holt.

Tattersal, I. (2012). *Masters of the planet: The search for our human origins.* NY: St. Martin's

Tuke, D. H. (1878). *Insanity in ancient and modern life, with chapters on its prevention.* London, Macmillan & Co.

Vanhaeren, M., d'Errico, F., Stringer, C., James, S., Todd, J. & Mienis, H. (2006). Middle Paleolithic shell beads in Israel and Algeria. *Science, 312*, 1785-1788.

Varky, A., & Brower, D. (2013). *Denial: Self-deception, false beliefs, and the origins of the human mind.* New York NY: Hachette Book Group.

Viet, L., & Nieder, A. (2013). Abstract rule neurons in the endbrain support intelligent behavior in corvid songbirds. *Nature Communications, 4* DOI: 10.1038/ ncomms3878.

Wallace, A. (1871). *Contributions to the theory of natural selection: A series of essays.* New York: Macmillan and Co.

Wilckens, K., Woo, S., Kirk, A., Erickson, K., & Wheeler, M. (2014). Role of sleep continuity and total sleep time in executive function across the adult lifespan. *Psychology and Aging, 29*, 658-665.

Chapter 3

Anthony, D. (2007). *The horse, the wheel, and language.* Princeton NJ: Princeton Univ. Press.

Coren, S. (2002). *The pawprints of history.* New York NY: Simon & Schuster.

Derr, M. (2011). *How the dog became the dog: From wolves to our best friends.* New York NY: Overlook Press.

D'Errico, F., Henshilwood, C., Lawson, G., Vanhaeren, M., Tillier, A., Soressi, M., Bresson, et al., (2003). Archaeological evidence for the emergence of language, symbolism, and music: An alternative multidisciplinary perspective. *Journal of World Prehistory, 17*, 1 – 70.

Dubuc, B. (2002). The origins of language. In *The brain from top to bottom*. Retrieved from http://thebrain.mcgill.ca

Gee, H. (2013). *The accidental species: Misunderstandings of human evolution*. Chicago IL: Chicago Univ. Press.

Groves, C. (1999). The advantages and disadvantages of being domesticated. *Perspectives on Human Biology, 4* (1), 1-12.

Hare, B. & Woods, V. (2013). *The genius of dogs: How dogs are smarter than you think*. New York NY: Penguin.

Hitchcock, D. (2015). *Tools of the stone age*. Retrieved from http://donsmaps.com/makingflinttools.html

Keddie, G. (1988). *The atlatl weapon*. Victoria BC: Royal British Columbia Museum.

Lippi, M., Foggi, B., Aranguren, B., Ronchitelli, A., & Revedin, A. (2015). Multistep food plant processing at Grotta Paglicci (Southern Italy) around 32,600 cal BP. *Proceedings of the U. S. National Academy of Sciences, 112,* 12075-12080.

Lopez, S., Munoz Ibanez, F., & Lerma, I. (2015). The Solutrean site of Ambrosia cave (Almeira, Spain). *Journal of Anthropological Research, 71,* 509-522.

McClellan, J. & Dorn, H. (2006). *Science and technology in world history: An introduction* (2nd ed.). Baltimore MD: John Hopkins U. Press.

O'Neill, D. (2013). *Early modern human culture*. Retrieved from anthro.palomar.edu/homo2/mod_homo_5.htm.

Paxton, D. (2000a). The case for a naturalistic perspective. *Anthrozoos, 13,* 5-8.

Revedin, A., Aranguren, B., Becattini, R., Longo, L., Marconi, E., Lippi, M., et al. (2010). Thirty thousand-year-old evidence of plant food processing. *Proceedings of the National Academy of Sciences, 107,* 18815–18819

Rice, P. (1999). On the origins of pottery. *Journal of Archaeological Method and Theory, 6* (1), 1-54.

Shipman, P. (2015). *The invaders: How humans and their dogs drove Neanderthals to extinction.* Cambridge MA: Harvard University Press.

Stringer, C. (2012). *Lone survivors: How we came to be the only humans on earth.* NY: Henry Holt.

Wayman, E. (2012). *Early bow and arrows offer insight into origins of human intellect.* Smithsonian.com, Nov. 7.

Wu, X., Zhang, C., Goldberg, P., Cohen, D., Pan, Y., Arpin, T., & Bar-Yosef, O. (2012). Early pottery at 20,000 years ago in Xianrendong Cave, China. *Science, 336* (6089), 696-700.

Chapter 4

Abel, T., Havekes, R., Saletin, J. & Walker, M. (2013). Sleep plasticity and memory from molecules to whole-brain networks. *Current Biology, 23,* 774-788.

Bourke-Taylor, H., Pallant, J., & Howie, L. (2012). Relationships between sleep disruptions, health and care responsibilities among mothers of school-aged children with disabilities. *Journal of Pediatrics and Child Health, 49,* 775-782.

Brown, E. & Low, C. (2008). Chaotic living conditions and sleep problems associated with children's responses to academic challenge. *Journal of Family Psychology, 22,* 920-923.

Burgard, S. (2011). The needs of others: Gender and sleep interruptions for caregivers. *Social Forces, 89,* 1189 – 1215.

Buysse, D., Reynolds, C., Monk, T., Berman, S., & Kupfer, D. (1989). The Pittsburgh Sleep Quality Index: A new instrument for psychiatric practice and research. *Psychiatry Research, 28,* 193-213.

Cirelli C., & Tononi, G. (2008). Is sleep essential? *PLoS Biol. 6*(8).

Collins, A. (2014). *Man's best hero: True stories of great American dogs.* Nashville TN: Abington Press.

Colter, T., & Altevogt, B. (2000). Functional and economic impact of sleep loss and sleep-related disorders. In *Sleep disorders and sleep deprivation: An unmet public health problem.* Washington DC: National Academies Press.

Cutts, D., Meyers, A., Black, M., Casey, P., Chilton, M., Cook, J., Geppert, J., et al., (2011). US housing insecurity and the health of very young children. *American Journal of Public Health, 101,* 1508 – 1514.

Duff, K. (2014). *The secret life of sleep.* New York NY: Simon & Schuster.

Ellenbogen, J., Hu, P., Payne. J., Titone, D., & Walker, W., (2007). Human relational memory requires time and sleep. *Proceedings of the National Academy of Sciences, 104,* 7723-7728.

Frank, M. G. (2006). The mystery of sleep function: Current perspectives and future directions. *Reviews in the Neurosciences, 17,* 375-392.

Hart, D., & Sussman, P. (2008). *Man the hunted: Primates, predators and human evolution.* Boulder CO: Westview Press.

Hemmingson, H., Stenhammar, A., & Paulson, K. (2008). Sleep problems and the need for parental night-time attention in children with physical disabilities. *Child Care, Health and Development, 35*, 89-95.

Hubpages.com (2013). *Sleeping habits of dogs.* Retrieved from <u>http://hubpages.com</u> /animals/Sleeping-Habits-of-Dogs.

Krueger, J., Rector, D., Van Dongen, H., Belenky, G., & Panksepp, J. (2008): Sleep is controlled at the local level, not centrally for the whole organism. *Nature Reviews Neuroscience, 9*, 910–919.

Levy-Vroelant, C. (2010). Housing vulnerable groups: The development of a new public action sector. *International Journal of Housing Policy, 10*, 443 – 456.

McCann, D., Bull, R., & Winzenberg, T. (2015). Sleep deprivation in parents caring for children with complex needs at home: A mixed methods systematic review. *Journal of Family Nursing, 21*, 86-118.

Nir, Y., & Tononi, G. (2010). Dreaming and the brain: From phenomenology to neurophysiology. *Trends in Cognitive Sciences, 14*, 88-100.

Oberg, G. (2011). The great recession's impact on children. Maternal and Child Health Journal, 15, 553-554.

Parish, S., Rose, R., Grinstein-Weiss, M., Richman, E. & Andrews, M. (2008). Material hardship in U. S. families raising children with disabilities. *Exceptional Children, 75*, 71-92.

Porkka-Heiskanen T. (1999). Adenosine in sleep and wakefulness. Annals of Medicine. 31, 125-129.

Randall, D. (2012). *Dreamland: Adventures in the strange science of sleep.* New York NY: Norton.

Rowbotham, M., Carroll, A., & Cuskelly, M. (2011). Mothers' and fathers' roles in caring for an adult child with an intellectual disability. *International Journal of Disability, Development and Education, 58*, 223-240.

Saletin, J., Golstein, A., & Walker, M. (2011). The role of sleep in directed forgetting and remembering of human memories. *Cerebral Cortex*, doi: 10.1093/cercor/bhr034.

Segnowski, T, & Delbruck, T. (2012). The language of the brain. *Scientific American, 307*, 54-59.

Siegel, J. M. (2005). Clues to the functions of mammalian sleep. *Nature, 437*, 1264-1271.

Singh, G. & Ghandour, R. (2012). Impact of neighborhood social conditions and household socioeconomic status on behavioral problems among US children. *Maternal and Child Health Journal, 16*, 158-169.

Snyder, G. (1990). *The practice of the wild*. SanFransisco CA: North Point Press.

Steele, R., & Davies, B. (2006). Impact in parents when a child has a progressive, life-threatening illness. *International Journal of Palliative Nursing, 12*, 576–585.

Steinbeck, J. (1954/2008) *Sweet Thursday*. NY: Penguin Classics.

Sterpenich, V., Schmidt, C., Albouy, G., Matarazzo, L., Vanhaudenhuyse, A., Boveroux, P., Delguelre, et al., (2015). Memory reactivation during REM sleep promotes its generalization and integration in cortical stores. *Sleep, 37* (6). Retrieved from http://dx.doi.org/10.5665/ sleep. 3762.

Stickgulo R. & Walker, M. (2006). Sleep, memory and plasticity. *Annual Review of Psychology, 57*, 139-166.

Swaminathan, N. (2008). Psychiatric disorders from no sleep? *Scientific American, 298* (1), 32-33.

Tononi, G. & Cirelli, C. (2006). Sleep function and synaptic homeostasis. *Sleep Medicine Reviews, 10,* 99-162.

Vandekerckhove, M., & Cluydts, R. (2010). The emotional brain and sleep: An intimate relationship. *Sleep Medicine Reviews, 14,* 219-226.

van der Halm, E., Yao, J., Sutt, S., Rao, V., Saletnm J. & Walker, M. (2011). REM sleep depotentiates amygdala activity to previous emotional experiences. *Current Biology, 21,* 2029-2032.

Wagner, U., Gals, S., Halder, H., Verleger, R., & Born, J. (2004). Sleep inspires insight. *Nature, 427,* 352-355.

Walker, M. (2006). Sleep to remember. *American Scientist, 94,* 326-333.

Chapter 5

Alpert, B. *The creative ice age brain: Cave art in the light of neuroscience.* Santa Fe NM: Foundation 20 21.

Barrett, D. (1993). The "committee of sleep": A study of dream incubation for problem solving. *Dreaming, 3,* 115-122.

Cherry, K. (2015) *Ten facts about dreams: What researchers have discovered about dreams.* Retrieved from http:// psychology.about.com/od/ statesofconsciousness/tp/ facts-about-dreams.htm

Collier, G. (2012). Dreams: Big and little. *Psychology Today.* Retrieved from https://www.psychologytoday.com /blog/ the-consciousness-question/201206/dreams-big-and-little.

Coren, S. (2002). *The pawprints of history.* New York NY: Simon & Schuster.

Crockford, S., & Kuzmin, Y. (2012). Comments on Germonpre et al. fossil dogs and wolves from paleolithic sites in Belgium, the Ukraine and Russia: Osteometry, ancient DNA and stable isotopes. *Journal of Archaeological Science, 39,* 2797–2801.

Duff, K. (2014). *The secret life of sleep.* New York NY: Simon & Schuster.

Griffith, R., trans. (1896). *The rig veda.* Retrieved from http://hinduwebsite.com/sacredscripts/rigintro.asp.

Horne, C. (2010). *The Vendidad: The Zoroastrian book of the law.* Whitefish, MT: Kessinger Publishing.

Hurd, R. (2008). *Big dreams and archetypal visions.* retrieved from http://dreamstudies.org/2008/11/14/big-dreams- archetypal-visions.

Irwin, L. (1992). Cherokee healing: Myth, dreams and medicine. *American Indian Quarterly, 16,* 237-257.

Irwin, L. (1994). Dreams, theory and culture: The Plains vision quest paradigm. *American Indian Quarterly, 18,* 229-245.

Jenkins, P. (2004). *Dream catchers: How mainstream America discovered native spirituality.* New York: Oxford University Press.

Kahn, D. (2007). Metacognition, recognition, and reflection while dreaming. In D. Barrett & P. McNamara (Eds.). *The new science of dreaming, Vol. 1.* (pp. 245-267). Westport CT: Praeger.

Lewis-Williams, D. (2002). *The mind in the cave: Consciousness and the origins of art.* London & New York: Thames and Hudson.

Lewis-Williams, D. & Pearce, D. (2005). *Inside the neolithic mind.* London & New York: Thames & Hudson.

Newby, J. (1997). The pact for survival: Humans and their animal companions. Sydney, AU: ABC Books.

Nicholson, P. (2010). The dog catacomb. *Archaeology, 63* (5), 34-34.

Nir, Y., & Tononi, G. (2010). Dreaming and the brain: From phenomenology to neurophysiology. *Trends in Cognitive Sciences, 14,* 88-100.

Papamichael, E. & Theochari, A. (2008). Artimedorus' Oneirocritica: Dream analysis in the Second Century. *Hellenic Psychiatry, 5*(2), 83-85.

Patton, K. (2004) "A great and strange correction": Intentionality, locality, and epiphany in the category of dream incubation. *History of Religions, 43,* 194-223.

Randall, D. (2012). *Dreamland: Adventures in the strange science of sleep.* New York NY: Norton.

Saredi, R., Baylor, G., Meier, B., & Strauch, I. (1997). Current concerns and REM-dreams: A laboratory study of dream incubation. *Dreaming, 7,* 195-208.

Semple, J. (1995). From paragon to pariah: Some reflections on human attitudes to dogs. In. J. Semple (Ed.) *The domestic dog: Its evolution, behavior, and interactions with people.* Cambridge UK: Cambridge Univ. Press.

Shipman, P. (2015). *The invaders: How humans and their dogs drove Neanderthals to extinction.* Cambridge MA: Harvard University Press.

Tedlock, B. (2005). *The woman in the shaman's body: Reclaiming the feminine in religion and medicine*. New York NY: Random House.

Wagner, U., Gals, S., Halder, H., Verleger, R., & Born, J. (2004). Sleep inspires insight. *Nature, 427,* 352-355.

Warren, C. (2013). *What the dog knows: Scent, science and the amazing ways dogs perceive the world*. New York NY: Simon & Schuster.

White, G., & Taytroe, L. (2003). Personal problem-solving using dream incubation: Dreaming, relaxation, or waking cognition? *Dreaming, 13,* 193-209.

Chapter 6

Anthony, D. (2007). *The horse, the wheel, and language*. Princeton NJ: Princeton Univ. Press.

Axelsson, E., Ratnakumar, A., Arendt, M., Maqbool, K., et al. (2013). The genomic signature of dog domestication reveals adaptation to a starch-rich diet. *Nature, 495,* 360-464.

Beaver, B. (2009). *Canine behavior: Insights and answers* (2nd Ed.). St. Louis MO: Elsevier.

Brottman, M. (2014). *The great Grisby: Two thousand years of literary, royal, philosophical, and artistic dog lovers and their exceptional animals*. New York NY: Harper Collins.

Crockford, S., & Kuzmin, Y. (2012). Comments on Germonpre et al. fossil dogs and wolves from paleolithic sites in Belgium, the Ukraine and Russia: Osteometry, ancient DNA and stable isotopes. *Journal of Archaeological Science, 39,* 2797–2801.

Dansey, W. & Arrian, F. (1831/2010). *Arrian on coursing: The Cynegeticus of the Younger Xenophon, translated from the Greek with classical and practical annotations and a brief sketch of the life and writings of the author.* LaVergne TN, BiblioLife.

Derr, M. (2011). *How the dog became the dog: From wolves to our best friends.* New York NY: Overlook Press.

Drake, A., Coquerelle, M., & Colombeau, G. (2015). 3D morphometric analysis of fossil canid skulls contradicts the suggested domestication of dogs during the late Paleolithic. *Nature, Scientific Reports, Article # 8299.*

Druzhkova, A., Thalmann, O, Trifonov, V., Leonard, J., Vorobieva, N., et al. (2013). Ancient DNA analysis affirms the canid from Altai as a primitive dog. *PLoS ONE 8*(3), e57754. doi:10.1371/journal.pone.0057754.

Germonpre, M., Laznickova, M, & Sablin, M. (2012). Paleolithic dog skulls at the Gravettian Predmosti site, the Czech Republic. *Journal of Archaeological Science, 39,* 2797–2801.

Germonpré, M., Sablin, M., Stevens, R., Hedges, R., Hofreiter, M., et al. (2009). Fossil dogs and wolves from paleolithic sites in Belgium, the Ukraine and Russia: Osteometry, ancient DNA and stable isotopes. *Journal of Archaeological Science 36,* 473–490.

Ghosh, P. (2015) DNA hints at earlier dog evolution. *BBC News,* May 21, 2015.

Goebel, T., Waters, M., & O'Rourke, D. (2008). The late pleistocene dispersal of modern humans in the Americas. *Science, 319,* 1497-1502.

Groomes, D., Clemons, A., Hulme, S., Kort, K. & Mesibov, G. (2014). Utilizing assistive dogs in integrated employment settings: Multidisciplinary elements to consider for individuals with ASD. *Journal of Vocational Rehabilitation, 40,* 165-173.

Groves, C. (1999). The advantages and disadvantages of being domesticated. *Perspectives on Human Biology, 4* (1), 1-12.

Hare, B. & Woods, V. (2013). *The genius of dogs: How dogs are smarter than you think.* New York NY: Penguin.

Harrington, S. (1999). Human footprints at Chauvet Cave. *Archaeology, 52* (5). Retrieved from http:// archive.archaeology. org/9909/newsbriefs/chauvet.html.

Larson, G., Karlsson, E., Perri, A., Webster, M., Ho, S., et al. (2012). Rethinking dog domestication by integrating genetics, archeology, and biogeography. *Proceedings of the National Academy of Sciences, 109,* 8878–8883.

Laughlin, C., & Rock, A. (2014). What can we learn from shamans' dreaming?: A cross-cultural exploration. *Dreaming, 24,* 23-252.

Lee, J. (2013). Dog and human genomes evolved together. *National Geographic News.* Retrieved 8/17/2015 from http:// news.nationalgeographic.com/news/ 2013/13/130514-dogs-domestication-humans-genome-science/

Masson, J. (2010). *The dog who couldn't stop loving.* New York NY: Harper Collins.

Morey, D. (2014). In search of Paleolithic dogs: A quest with mixed results. *Journal of Archaeological Science, 52,* 300-307.

Morey, D., & Wiant, M. (1992). Early holocene domestic dog burials from the North American Midwest. *Current Anthropology 33,* 225-229.

Nagasawa, M., Mitsui, S., En, S., Ohtani, N., Ohta, M., Sakuma, Y., Onaka, T., et al., (2015). Oxytocin-gaze positive loop and the coevolution of human-dog bonds. *Science, 348,* 333-336.

Newby, J. (1997). *The pact for survival: Humans and their animal companions*. Sydney, AU: ABC Books.

Patton, K. (2004) "A great and strange correction": Intentionality, locality, and epiphany in the category of dream incubation. *History of Religions, 43*, 194-223.

Paxton, D. (2000a). The case for a naturalistic perspective. *Anthrozoos, 13*, 5-8.

Shipman, P. (2015). *The invaders: How humans and their dogs drove Neanderthals to extinction*. Cambridge MA: Harvard University Press.

Skoglund, P., Ersmark, E., Palkopoulou, E., & Dalen, L. (2015). Ancient wolf genome reveals an early divergence of domestic dog ancestors and admixture into high-latitude breeds. *Current Biology, 25*, 1515-1519.

Stringer, C. (2012). *Lone survivors: How we came to be the only humans on earth*. NY: Henry Holt.

Thalmann, O., Shapiro, B., Cui, P., Schuenemann, V., et al. (2013). Complete mitochondrial genomes of ancient canids suggest a European origin of domestic dogs. *Science, 342*, 871-874.

Wilson, D. & Reeder, D. (2005). *Mammal species of the world* (3rd Ed.) Baltimore MD: Johns Hopkins Univ. Press.

Zak, P. (2014). *Dogs (and Cats) can love*. The Atlantic. Retrieved from http://www.the atlantic.com/ health/ archive/2014/04/ does-your-dog-or-cat-actually-love-you/360784.

Chapter 7

Brown, J. (2015). *Sanctuary of Asklepios, Epidaurus.* University of Warwick. Retrieved from http://www2. warwick.ac.uk/fac/arts/classics/students/modules/greek religion/database/clumcc.

Coren, S. (2002). *The pawprints of history.* New York NY: Simon & Schuster.

Dansey, W. & Arrian, F. (1831/2010). *Arrian on coursing: The Cynegeticus of the Younger Xenophon, translated from the Greek with classical and practical annotations and a brief sketch of the life and writings of the author.* LaVergne TN, BiblioLife.

Derr, M. (2011). *How the dog became the dog: From wolves to our best friends.* New York NY: Overlook Press.

Dog Breed Information Center (2015). *Understanding a dog's senses.* Retrieved 7/8/2015 from http://www.dogbreed info.com/articles/dogsenses.

Dog.com (2015). *Dog sense of smell.* Retrieved 7/8/2015 from http://www.dog.com/dog-articles/dog-sense-of-smell/2054/.

DogHealth.com (2015). *Hearing in dogs.* Retrieved 10/14/2015 from http://www.doghealth.com/ears/ hearing-in-dogs.

Duff, K. (2014). *The secret life of sleep.* New York NY: Simon & Schuster.

Gazzaniga, M. (2008). *Human: The science behind what makes us unique.* NY: Harper-Collins.

Goodavage, M. (2012). *Seven amazing facts about your dog's sense of smell.* Retrieved 7/8/2015 from http:// www.dogster.com/lifestyle/dog-facts-sense-of-smell.

Hare, B. & Woods, V. (2013). *The genius of dogs: How dogs are smarter than you think.* New York NY: Penguin.

Kidd, R. (2004). *Getting to the source of the dog's ability to smell.* Retrieved 7/8/2015 from http://www.whole-dog-journal.com/ issues/7_11/features/Canine-Sense-of-Smell_15668-1.

Maguire, S. (2015). *Dog senses.* Retrieved 10/14/2015 from http:// www.dogbreedinfo.com/articles/dogsenses.htm.

Masson, J. (2010). *The dog who couldn't stop loving.* New York NY: Harper Collins.

Miklosi, A., Kubinyi, E., Topal, J., Gacsi, M., Viranyi, Z., & Csanyi, V. (2003) A simple reason for a big difference: Wolves do not look back at humans but dogs do. *Current Biology, 13,* 763.

Newby, J. (1997). *The pact for survival: Humans and their animal companions.* Sydney, AU: ABC Books.

Pavlov, I. (1927). *Conditioned reflexes: An investigation of the physiological activity of the cerebral cortex* (G.V. Anrep, trans.) London: Oxford University Press.

Shipman, P. (2015). *The invaders: How humans and their dogs drove Neanderthals to extinction.* Cambridge MA: Harvard University Press.

Udell, M., Dorey, N., & Wynne, C. (2010). What did domestication do to dogs? A new account of dogs' sensitivity to human actions. *Biological Reviews, 85,* 327-345.

Udell, M., Dorey, N., & Wynne, C. (2011). Can your dog read your mind? Understanding the causes of canine perspective taking. *Learning and Behavior, 39,* 289-302.

Udell, M. & Wynne, C. (2011). Reevaluating canine perspective taking behavior. *Learning and Behavior, 39,* 318-232.

Chapter 8

Asher L., Diesel, G., Summers, J., McGreevy, P., & Collins, L. (2009). Inherited defects in pedigree dogs: Disorders related to breed standards. *Veterinary Journal, 182,* 402-411.

Auxier, R. (2008). The varieties of canine experience. In S. Hales (Ed.) *What philosophy can tell you about your dog* (pp. 215-235). Peru IL: Carus Publishing.

Bellumori, T., Famula, T., Bannasch, D., Belanger, J., & Oberbauer, A. (2013). Prevalence of inherited disorders among mixed-breed and purebred dogs. *Journal of the American Veterinary Medical Association, 242,* 1549-1555.

Brown, J. (2015). *Sanctuary of Asklepios, Epidaurus.* University of Warwick. Retrieved from http://www2.warwick. ac.uk/fac/arts/classics/students/modules/greekreligion/ database/clumcc.

Coren, S. (2002). *The pawprints of history.* New York NY: Simon & Schuster.

Dansey, W. & Arrian, F. (1831/2010). *Arrian on coursing: The Cynegeticus of the Younger Xenophon, translated from the Greek with classical and practical annotations and a brief sketch of the life and writings of the author.* LaVergne TN, BiblioLife.

Derr, M. (2011). *How the dog became the dog: From wolves to our best friends.* New York NY: Overlook Press.

Gazzaniga, M. (2008). *Human: The science behind what makes us unique.* NY: Harper-Collins.

Grey, T. (1995). *Wagner's musical prose: Texts and contexts*. New York: Cambridge Univ. Press.

Louv, R. (2008). *Last child in the woods: Saving our children from nature-deficit disorder*. Chapel Hill NC: Algonquin.

Masson, J. (2010). *The dog who couldn't stop loving*. New York NY: Harper Collins.

Newby, J. (1997). *The pact for survival: Humans and their animal companions*. Sydney, AU: ABC Books.

Patterson, C., (2002). *Eternal Treblinka: Our treatment of animals and the holocaust*. New York NY: Lantern Books.

Shipman, P. (2015). *The invaders: How humans and their dogs drove Neanderthals to extinction*. Cambridge MA: Harvard University Press.

Swanson, K. (2008). Witches, children and Kiva-the-research-dog: Striking problems encountered in the field. *Area, 40*, 55-64.

Warren, C. (2013). *What the dog knows: Scent, science and the amazing ways dogs perceive the world*. New York NY: Simon & Schuster.

Chapter 9

Adkins, K. (2008). Humanity is a prejudice. In S. Hales (Ed.) *What philosophy can tell you about your dog* (pp. 237-248). Peru IL: Carus Publishing.

American Kennel Club (2015). *Where do dogs sleep at night?* Retrieved from http://www.akc.org/akc-dog-lovers/ where-do-dogs-sleep-at-night.

Auxier, R. (2008). The varieties of canine experience. In S. Hales (Ed.) *What philosophy can tell you about your dog* (pp. 215-235). Peru IL: Carus Publishing.

Berry, A., Borgi, M., Franca, N., Alleva, E., & Cirulli, F. (2013). Use of assistance and therapy dogs for children with autism spectrum disorders: A critical review of the current evidence. *Journal of Alternative and Complementary Medicine, 19* (2), 73-80.

Brainyquote (2001-2016) *Diogenes quotes.* Retrieved from http://www.brainyquote.com/quotes/authors/d/diogenes.html.

Brooks, D. (2015), *The evolution of simplicity.* New York Times, Nov. 3, p. A29.

Brottman, M. (2014). *The great Grisby: Two thousand years of literary, royal, philosophical, and artistic dog lovers and their exceptional animals.* New York NY: Harper Collins.

Bureau of ATF (2018). *Explosives detection canines.* Retrieved 5/27/2018 from https://www.atf.gov/about/explosives-detection-canines.

Collins, A. (2014). *Man's best hero: True stories of great American dogs.* Nashville TN: Abington Press.

Dansey, W. & Arrian, F. (1831/2010). *Arrian on coursing: The Cynegeticus of the Younger Xenophon, translated from the Greek with classical and practical annotations and a brief sketch of the life and writings of the author.* LaVergne TN, BiblioLife.

Douglas, H. (2008). What I learned from my dogs about being an animal. In S. Hales (Ed.) *What philosophy can tell you about your dog* (pp. 145-153). Peru IL: Carus Publishing.

Dyer, C. (2013) The Aboriginal people in Sydney as seen by Eugene Delessert, December 1844 to August 1845. *Aboriginal History, 37,* 93 - 110.

Freud, S. (1917/1986). A difficulty in the path of psychoanalysis. In J. Strachey (Ed.) *The standard edition of the complete psychological works of Sigmund Freud. Vol. XVII* (1917-1919), pp. 135-144. New York NY: W. W. Norton.

Gabor, G. (2008). What Aristotle can teach you about your dog. In. S. Hales (Ed.) *What philosophy can tell you about your dog* (pp. 271-282). Peru IL: Carus Publishing.

Groomes, D., Clemons, A., Hulme, S., Kort, K. & Mesibov, G. (2014). Utilizing assistive dogs in integrated employment settings: Multidisciplinary elements to consider for individuals with ASD. *Journal of Vocational Rehabilitation, 40,* 165-173.

Hare, B. & Woods, V. (2013). *The genius of dogs: How dogs are smarter than you think.* New York NY: Penguin.

Levinson, B. (1962). The dog as co-therapist. *Mental Hygiene, 46,* 59-65.

Lit, L., Schweitzer, J. & Oberbauer, A. (2011). Handler beliefs affect scent detection dog outcomes. *Animal cognition, 14,* 387-394.

Lobell, J. & Powell, E. (2010). More than man's best friend. *Archaeology, 63* (5), 26-35.

Losey, R., Bazaliski, V., Garvie-Lok, S., Germonpre, M., Leonard, J., et al. (2011). Canids as persons: Early neolithic dog and wolf burials, Cis-Baikal, Siberia. *Journal of Anthropological Archaeology, 30,* 174-189.

Miller, A. (2015). How we mourn our dead pets. *Literary Hub,* retrieved from http://lithub.com/how-we-mourn-our-dead-pets.

Morey, D., & Wiant, M. (1992). Early holocene domestic dog burials from the North American Midwest. *Current Anthropology 33,* 225-229.

Newby, J. (1997). *The pact for survival: Humans and their animal companions.* Sydney, AU: ABC Books.

New York Times (Feb. 28, 1944). *Medals for everybody, 43,* #9.

Orlean, S. (2011). The dog star. *The New Yorker,* Aug. 29.

Payne, E., Bennett, P., & McGreevy, P. (2015). Current perspectives on attachment and bonding in the dog-human dyad. *Psychology Research and Behavior Management, 8,* 71-79.

Santaniello, W. (2008). Bitches gone wild: On canine liberty. In S. Hales (Ed.) *What philosophy can tell you about your dog* (pp. 31-44). Peru IL: Carus Publishing.

Schinkel, A. (2008). Dog dignity. In S. Hales (Ed.) *What philosophy can tell you about your dog* (pp. 248-258). Peru IL: Carus Publishing.

Solomon, O. (2010). What a dog can do: Children with autism and therapy dogs in social interaction. *Ethos, 38* (1), 143-166).

Stamatellos, G. (2009). *Cynics.* Retrieved 10/16/2015 from http://philosophy.gr/ hellinistic/cynics.htm

Statile, G. Two canine dogmas: Language and love. In S. Hales (Ed.) *What philosophy can tell you about your dog* (pp. 63-74). Peru IL: Carus Publishing.

Stetina, B., Turner, K., Burger, E., Glenk, L., McElheney, J. Handlos, U., & Kothgassner, O. (2011). Learning emotion recognition from canines? Two for the road. *Journal of Veterinary Behavior: Clinical Applications and Research, 6,* 108-114.

Thompson, B. (2012). *Sgt. Stubby*. Retrieved 7/30/15 from http:// www. badassoftheweek.com/sgtstubby.html.

Vyasa, K. (Trans. K. M. Ganguli, 1883-1896). The Mahabharata. http://www.sacred-texts.com/hin/maha.

Chapter 10

Adkins, K. (2008). Humanity is a prejudice. In S. Hales (Ed.) *What philosophy can tell you about your dog* (pp. 237-248). Peru IL: Carus Publishing.

Blair, J., Mitchell, D., & Blair, K. (2005). *The psychopath: Emotion and the brain*. Malden MA: Blackwell.

Brottman, M. (2014). *The great Grisby: Two thousand years of literary, royal, philosophical, and artistic dog lovers and their exceptional animals*. New York NY: Harper Collins

Clarke, W. N. (2004). *Person and being*. Milwaukee WI: Marquette University Press.

Coren, S. (2002). *The pawprints of history*. New York NY: Simon & Schuster.

DeGrazia, D. (2002). Are we essentially persons? Olson, Baker, and a reply. *The Philosophical Forum, 31*, 101-120.

DeGrazia, D. (2009). Self-awareness in animals. In R. Lurz (Ed.) *The philosophy of animal minds* (pp. 201-217). Cambridge UK: Cambridge Univ. Press

Dennett, D. (1996). *Kinds of minds: Toward an understanding of consciousness*. New York NY: Basic Books.

Duhau, L. (2008). What thoughts can your dog think? In S. Hales (Ed.) *What philosophy can tell you about your dog* (pp. 75-84). Peru IL: Carus Publishing.

Gabor, G. (2008). What Aristotle can teach you about your dog. In. S. Hales (Ed.) *What philosophy can tell you about your dog* (pp. 271-282). Peru IL: Carus Publishing.

Glenn, A., Raine, A., & Schug, R. (2009). The neural correlates of moral decision-making in psychopathy. *Molecular Psychiatry, 14*, 5-6.

Hare, B. & Woods, V. (2013). *The genius of dogs: How dogs are smarter than you think.* New York NY: Penguin.

Krause, S. (2010). Moral sentiment and the politics of human rights. *The art of theory: Conversations in political philosophy.* Retrieved 8/14/2

Lee, W. (2008). "Who is my special beagle?" In S. Hales (Ed.) *What philosophy can tell you about your dog* (pp. 259-272). Peru IL: Carus Publishing.

Losey, R., Bazaliski, V., Garvie-Lok, S., Germonpre, M., Leonard, J., et al. (2011). Canids as persons: Early neolithic dog and wolf burials, Cis-Baikal, Siberia. *Journal of Anthropological Archaeology, 30*, 174-189.

Mazis, G. (2008). Our embodied friendships with dogs. In S. Hales (Ed.) *What philosophy can tell you about your dog* (pp. 115-134). Peru IL: Carus Publishing.

Nagasawa, M., Mitsui, S., En, S., Ohtani, N., Ohta, M., Sakuma, Y., Onaka, T., Mogi, K. & Kitusui, T. (2015). Oxytocin-gaze positive loop and the coevolution of human-dog bonds. *Science, 348*, 333-336.

Newby, J. (1997). *The pact for survival: Humans and their animal companions*. Sydney, AU: ABC Books.

Payne, E., Bennett, P., & McGreevy, P. (2015). Current perspectives on attachment and bonding in the dog-human dyad. *Psychology Research and Behavior Management, 8,* 71-79.

Pepperberg, I. (2009). *Alex and me: How a scientist and a parrot discovered a hidden world of animal intelligence – and formed a deep bond*. New York: Harper-Collins.

Range, F., Horn. L., Viranyi, Z., & Huber, L. (2009). The absence of reward induces inequity aversion in dogs. *Proceedings of the National Academy of Sciences, 106,* 340-346.

Santaniello, W. (2008). Bitches gone wild: On canine liberty. In S. Hales (Ed.) *What philosophy can tell you about your dog* (pp. 31-44). Peru IL: Carus Publishing.

Wittgenstein, L. (1945). *Philosophical investigations.* (3rd Ed.). Oxford, UK: Basil, Blackwell & Mott.

ACKNOWLEDGEMENTS

I am grateful to the scholars and scientists who provided valuable information to help with my search for material: Pat Shipman, David DeGrazia, Sharon Krause, Stanley Coren and Abby Grace Drake, and to Mary Burch for reinforcing for me the importance of thorough scholarship. Thanks to the people who read through and commented on sections of the book: Susan Hagner, Katherine Hagner, Mary Schuh and Julie Moser. Thanks to Eric Post for keeping the math straight. Thanks to the folks at the Freud Museum in Vienna and the Smithsonian Museum of American History for their helpful assistance, and to AuthorHouse and especially Bill Overman for helping put everything together.

PICTURE CREDITS

1. *Sigmund Freud and Jofi, 1937*

   Photo by Photo12/UIG. Hulton Archive. Courtesy Getty Images

2. *Early Stone Hand-Axes*

   Left: Photo by Madsci. Right: Photo by J. Gaunin. iStock Collection. Courtesy ThinkStock

3. *Blade-Flaked Stone Point*

   Photo by Wlad74. iStock Collection. Courtesy ThinkStock

4. *Atlatl Throwers*

   Photo by Richard Hook. Corbis Collection. Courtesy Getty Images

5. *Late Paleolithic Bone Tools*

   Photo by G. Dagli Orti. De Angelis Collection. Courtesy Getty Images

6. *Venus Figurine*

   Photos.com Collection. Courtesy ThinkStock

7. *The Big Bad Wolf Disguised as Grandma*

   Photo by J. C. Rosemann. Engraving by Adrian Ludwig Richter. Courtesy Getty Images

8. *The Temples and Cult of Asclepius, from "The History of Medicine" series by Robert Thom.*

   From the collection of Michigan Medicine, University of Michigan, Gift of Pfizer, Inc., UMHS.5

9. *Beware of Dog Mosaic, Ruins of Pompeii*

   Photo by Laura DiBiase. iStock Collection. Courtesy ThinkStock

10. *Poco Defending the Front Door against All Enemies, Foreign, Domestic, and Imaginary*

    Photo by the Author

11. *Face Time: Osiris and Anubis*

    Photo by Fotografia Basica. Courtesy Getty Images

12. *Artemis, Goddess of the Hunt, and Companion*

    Photo by Duncan1890. Courtesy Getty Images

13. *Searching for Earthquake Survivors*

    Photo by millionhope. iStock collection. Courtesy Getty Images

14. *Greyfriar's Bobby*

    Photo by Jenntakespictures. iStock collection. Courtesy Getty Images

15. *Sgt. Stubby, in Uniform, Awarded Medal by Gen. Pershing*

   Smithsonian Museum of American History. Used with Permission

16. *Rin-Tin-Tin Gets Top Billing*

   Warner Bros. Movie Poster, in the public domain

17. *Friends Playing at Dog Park.*

   Photo by Darwin Brandis. iStock collection. Courtesy Getty Images